Pick of Punch

PICK OF

PUNCH

PUNCH and HUTCHINSON of London

A Punch book, published by Punch Publications Limited
in association with
Hutchinson & Co. (*Publishers*) Ltd.
3 Fitzroy Square, London W.1
London   Melbourne   Sydney   Auckland
Wellington   Johannesburg   Cape Town
and agencies throughout the world
Printed in Great Britain by
Hazell Watson & Viney Ltd., Aylesbury
Buckinghamshire
ISBN 0 09 109920 X

Contents

Introduction

Journalism, Chesterton once said, largely consists of saying "Lord Jones is dead" to people who never even knew he was alive. True enough; death is drama, and drama sells papers. There is much to be said for the argument that the world hasn't really got any worse: it's just that the news coverage has got so much better.

A year ago, a publisher in Sacramento launched America's first-ever newspaper devoted exclusively to good news. It listed share prices, but only those that had gone up. It reported that, in the previous year, 197,000,000 American did not commit a crime; 4,987,000 college students took no part in riots and demonstrations, and 201,000,000 Americans did not use illegal drugs. *Punch* has not gone that far, but we have certainly tried to show that this is not such a gloomy age as Fleet Street and Television would like everyone to think. We've had a lot of fun in the process and a number of contributions to the cause are featured in this year's *Pick of Punch*.

Everyone claims to have a sense of humour: it's something we all take for granted. But an astonishingly large number of people get angry when they sense that the humorist is laughing at them, and at the things they believe in. Their idea of humour is to have comedians make fools of themselves on TV. This is why we are frequently told that some article or cartoon is "in bad taste" or "irresponsible". We don't apologise: *Punch* tries to draw its humour from the comedy of our surroundings and believes that the best definition of a sense of humour is the ability to laugh at oneself. And if this makes you feel that some of us take our humour seriously—well, you are dead right. We like to think, though, that you'll feel a little happier after reading this volume.

WILLIAM DAVIS

Nothing is Ever Right

By WILLIAM DAVIS

One of the more libellous complaints made about the British is that they don't complain enough. The charge was repeated the other day in the Daily Mail. "The fact is," said one of the paper's writers, "that we do want something better, but we're too damn lazy to demand it."

I protest. I express grief, pain, censure. I grumble and beef, lament and dissent. For this is not a true picture of us at all.

We complain all the time. About the weather, the young, the old, the roads, the Government, the Opposition, the food, the balance of payments, the radio, the French, the unions, the trains, the beaches, the Irish, the beer, the taxes, the shops, the blacks, the telephone, the schools, the tea . . . and anything else we can think of. There are even people, believe it or not, who complain about the things we say in Punch. In short, nothing is ever right.

What *could* be argued, though, is that we don't take this complaining business seriously enough. There is no determination, no sense of achievement; no pride, no pleasure. We are easily rebuffed; confronted with a French waiter, the average Briton is as spineless as spaghetti. In France, complaining is a way of life. In Britain, it is a side-show. The only national figure we have ever produced is Disgusted of Tunbridge Wells; in France they created de Gaulle, and in America they have

1942

*"Calm yourself, dear. Even Hitler can't be both dregs **and** scum."*

9

1902

A SECRET OF THE SEA

Passenger: "*Look here, steward, if this is coffee, I want tea; but if this is tea, then I wish for coffee.*"

produced Ralph Nader. We are amateurs playing against professionals. This, I submit, will have to change. There is no room in the new Britain, the Better Tomorrow, for curates who eat rotten eggs.

The first thing to realise is that complaining requires certain basic skills. Some people are born to it, but most of us need practice. Expert complaining calls for great strength of character. It is so easy to go soft; to recognise the value of the other man's argument, and to be duped into thinking that (a) life is short (b) he didn't mean any harm and (c) he needs his job. The real professional recognises that all other men are incompetent fools, and that blessed are the strong etcetera.

Women are, on the whole, better at this than men. Women instinctively know that nothing is ever right; they'd find fault even in paradise. (*That* should be good for at least fifty complaining letters.)

Fleet Street leader writers also have a rudimentary understanding of what is required. The job teaches you to acknowledge certain absolute truths. Governments make a mess of everything, regardless of their colour. World affairs are childishly simple, and would present no problem at all if people stopped behaving like, well, people. Bureaucrats are bureaucrats are bureaucrats. Railways are badly run, and would still be badly run if you threw out the present management and put in Ted Heath, Charles Clore, Arnold Weinstock, McKinseys, and the entire Board of Marks and Spencer. Exports will never be what they should be. And no waiter, cook, taxman, shop assistant, Minister, manufacturer, salesman, teacher, civil servant, broadcaster or humorist ever does his job properly. Once you appreciate this, professional complaining becomes a lot easier. You can confidently eliminate those ifs and buts, and put the world on the correct course.

It helps, of course, to be a creative worrier. If you are happy, you will never make a good complainer. Happiness is complacency; worrying is dynamic. Try to worry

more about the future; learn to be miserable about things that have yet to happen. Make a list of things to worry about this weekend.

Do you lie awake at night, worrying about the Sultan of Oman's slaves?

Do you feel like smashing up your neighbour's furniture in protest against pollution?

Would you stay away from work tomorrow, to show your disapproval of the Government's policy in Anguilla?

No? Just as I thought. When it comes down to it, you're as nervous as a turkey in November. It won't do.

Perhaps we ought to start more gently. St. Pancras Station, after all, wasn't built in a day. Don't be content, tomorrow morning, with complaining to your wife, travel companion, or chum at the office, about the 8.27 being late—and then promptly forgetting all about it. Telling friends is cheating; it doesn't count. They will be unduly sympathetic, partly because they want you to buy another round, and partly because they want you to listen to *their* complaints once you've finished. And don't write to the General Manager of the guilty region; professional complainers don't risk ending up in waste paper baskets.

Raise hell. Don't be satisfied until everyone in the office feels as belligerent as you, and until the region's railwaymen come out on strike in protest against your protest. Remember the wise words of Josh Billings: "the wheel that squeaks the loudest is the one that gets the grease."

After this, you should be able to move on to higher things. The BBC, the Post Office, and Punch are natural targets—and satisfaction is guaranteed, providing you obey a few simple rules.

Don't write to the BBC to complain about the BBC; write to the Post Office or Punch. Similarly, don't write to Punch to complain about Punch; write to the BBC.

1948

"Furthermore, we must face up to the unpleasant fact that as we've had no strikes we must have been grossly overpaying our workers."

1949

"Could I change it? I find my husband already has one."

Don't complain about the big, obvious mistakes. Concentrate on the little ones which everyone else has missed. The late Lord Beaverbrook found this most effective: he terrified subordinates by spotting the tiny cock-ups which they were sure had been completely overlooked, and in so doing ensured the maximum degree of pleasure.

Don't use polite language: there is nothing wrong with good, honest abuse. And don't on any account add phrases like "I am, Sir, your obedient servant." Could you see a Frenchman doing anything so absurd?

Don't accept excuses or explanations of any kind. There is no excuse for anything: "an excuse is a lie guarded."

While you're doing this, you might try three useful little exercises.

The first is known as "torturing the waiter." It's a good test—a sort of "A" level—because waiters tend to have a high resistance line. The secret here is to emulate the Spanish matador: pick a young, relatively experienced bull.

Having found him, do not on any account use any of the obvious ploys. Resist the urge to tell him that the fly in your soup is "extremely well cooked." Don't ask him if they serve indigestion tablets with every course, or whether any of his customers ever come again. He's heard them all before, even if he is just eighteen, and he'll be snappy on the comebacks. Above all, don't tell him that you are a personal friend of the owner/manager. That's just asking for trouble. He knows the owner/manager won't fire him, because staff is hard to come by nowadays, and that you are not going to embarrass your personal friend by making a fuss in front of all the customers. In other words, he's safe.

It's much more effective to order something he has to make at your table, such as Steak Diane or Crêpe Suzette, and to knock the whole thing over at a crucial moment. If he keeps his temper, the round goes to him. If he doesn't, you try again.

12

This time, you announce in a loud voice, that you're the food critic of the Flame-thrower's Gazette and that you know the restaurant is good, but that the service can be awful if you get the wrong waiter. If he is French or Italian, he will be much too proud to let anyone think that *he* is the wrong waiter. So you have him at your mercy. While he serves the first course, tell everyone in earshot that French/Italian football teams are awful—that they give failure a bad name. It takes remarkable will-power to stand up to *that*, and the chances are that he will drop the entire hors d'oeuvre into your lap. Victory! Now you can *really* complain.

The second exercise is known as "hounding the shop assistant." Here again a subtle approach is needed to ensure maximum satisfaction. Don't walk into a fish shop and say "these aren't crabs, they're spiders." She will probably agree with you. It's much better to ask her to cut up, say, a fresh salmon, and then change your mind. If it doesn't work the first time, try again. Sooner or later she'll explode—and then you can make your scene.

The third exercise is called "talking about the boss." Everyone does it; even the boss talks about *his* boss. Only the amateur, however, provides ammunition for both his rivals and his victim by complaining, say, about his decision to promote some young fool to a senior job. Better to encourage others to complain, and to complain to him about their complaints. If you see what I mean.

There are countless other ways of turning yourself into an expert complainer: baiting the postman, tormenting the traffic warden, harassing politicians. The past is your most useful ally; one reason why nothing is ever right is that nothing is as good as it used to be. Try to meet like-minded citizens and organise complaint-evenings. Make a point of reading only the bad news in your paper—it shouldn't be too difficult—and of ignoring the few TV programmes which pretend that it is possible to be happy. Given a choice of two calamities, choose both. And make complaining *pay*. I once knew a stockbroker who made a comfortable living by going along to annual company meetings, raising hell, and then accepting fat commissions from the frightened Board of Directors in return for a promise to keep quiet in future.

From time to time you may feel tempted to praise someone who appears to have given you good service. *Don't do it*. Look for a flaw, however small, and *complain*. It may happen, too, that someone will one day get it into his head to complain about *you*. There are people, it seems, who don't like to listen to one's favourite gramophone records at 2 a.m. Don't just brush them aside; complain about their lack of cultural understanding, and their stupid failure to soundproof the walls and ceilings of their flats. Register your protest by turning up the volume.

Persevere. Find a little bad in the best of things. With luck, you may end up like the chap on this week's cover—a man secure in the certainty that, in this world at least, nothing is ever right.

1953

"It looks like being the worst year on record unless we get some rain . . .

. . . sun . . .

. . . rain, pretty soon."

SERVICE GAME

by Graham

"We've got to get the parts down from the works, of course—if the strike's over that is, then I've two of the lads on holiday, so we're a bit pushed. Let's see now, this is Wednesday . . ."

"There's your trouble."

"Look, why not just leave this to me, sir."

"Then just after the high-pitched whining stopped, steam started coming out of the ash-tray."

"This'll be the engine, I suppose."

"I was promised it for four thirty!"

"You're **sure** you only brought it in for a wash and polish?"

'It was going like a bird till you gave it a tune-up!'

"It was when we were adjusting the track rod length to get the expansion slot registering with the clamp joint, that we found the play in your worm screw bearing."

O Death Where is Thy Sting-a-ling-a-ling

Vincent Mulchrone laughs all the way to the grave

The first bribe I ever took as a reporter was a half-a-crown. I was seventeen, and he was dead.

"Would you like to have a look at him?" the widow asked. Office instructions on the point were explicit. I looked.

The other women in the little West Riding kitchen gathered round as the handkerchief was lifted from his face for the umpteenth time.

He was my first corpse, and for the first time I heard what was to become a familiar litany—"Ee, doesn't he look lovely? . . . Better in death than in life, Sarah Jane . . . Doesn't he look like himself?"

I was backing out when the widow reached under the tea caddy on the mantelpiece and handed me the half-dollar. I composed my pimply features and explained that there was no fee. This, I said, was journalism.

But I must take it. *He* had left it for me. But he didn't know me. She knew that.

"Before he died," she explained "he said 'When I've gone, they'll be sending somebody round from t'Observer. Tell him to have a pint wi' me—and tell him to get t'bloody thing right.'"

By chance I came across his funeral tea. They were burying him with ham at the Co-op Hall. There was tea—great, steaming, practically untouched urns of it.

The Co-op was run by Primmers, but the janitor wasn't one, and winked an eye at the bottles smuggled in from the pub over the road. The therapy stopped short of a knees-up. But I've been to worse *parties*.

The feast was splendid. The widow, who conceded that I'd "got it right," explained that, as well as the insurance, she'd had him in a club. There are still scores of burial clubs listed with the Registrar of Friendly

16

most mourners have never seen before and may never see again.

He will officiate for as little as a guinea. The only briefing he needs if the crematorium, too, is strange, is on the location of the button that will send old Fred sliding stage Right to the Gas Board's special pride.

The great majority of those who go—600,000 of us every year—no longer believe in that damnation which gave point to the fear of death. Why, then, the antiseptic ritual, the bottling of emotions, the conspiracy to pretend that death has not occurred and nobody is grieving?

Death, it seems, has superseded sex as the last taboo. In his book *Death, Grief and Mourning*, Geoffrey Gorer convincingly concluded . . . "death and mourning are treated with much the same prudery as sexual impulses were a century ago."

Certainly our squeamishness about death and the mechanics of disposing of the body is utterly irrational. We try to deny the facts of death and loss. The Victorian

Societies, survivors of hundreds started in Lancashire early in the nineteenth century to avoid a pauper's grave and provide a bit of a do for the mourners.

The Friendly Funeral Society, founded 1815, offered the relatives a benefit of 48s.—and 2s. more "provided they have beer to the amount of 4s. where the collecting box is." The link between pubs and funerals is an old one.

A funeral used to be an occasion, sometimes grand, sometimes boozy, generally a great display but always, one might almost say, full of life. Corpses were always "beautiful," funerals always "lovely." Now it's twenty-five minutes at the crematorium (and a "fine" if the clergyman runs over time), a peek at the flowers on the way to the gate, and a cup of tea in the parlour.

Where we used to see them off with ham, now we do it with high speed gas. An ad. in the funeral trade press says "High Speed Gas—chosen by over ninety-six per cent of Britain's crematoria." Where, one wonders, are the leisurely four per cent?

A man used to lie in his own church and be buried in his own churchyard. Now the body goes to a "chapel of rest" and its disposal becomes an embarrassing sanitary exercise set to Muzak.

Well, say the undertakers—3,500 of them run a £60 million-a-year industry—we offer chapels of rest because vicars can't afford to heat churches for just a few hours.

And because so many families are out of touch with the church the undertakers frequently hire a clergyman

"Who's a pretty boy, then?"

17

convention of giving up social activities for a time has almost gone. Unlike mourners in Europe, we have stopped wearing full mourning.

"Must keep busy," we say. "Think of the future. Life must go on." Occasionally the dead themselves anticipate this and insist on paying for a last round for the boys from the coffin.

An old Yorkshireman recently left instructions for his cortège to stop outside the George and Dragon, where he had left a fiver for the purpose. Said his son "As he was a happy man who looked on this as his last joke, we played it out."

Andre Simon, the wine writer, ordered champagne for his memorial service. A Cheshire publisher arranged his own funeral stag party. His son said "Father had a wonderful sense of humour."

Old men, you see, with a glint in their eye, and memories of funerals as they used to be. The publisher expressly directed that there should be no wailing women at his funeral.

A Halifax widow, certainly no boozer, felt so strongly about the misery of modern funerals that she forbade mourners to come near hers. Instead, said her Will "... after my coffin has been removed I want my friends and neighbours to drink three bottles of champagne, provided by me."

Not that drink is essential to give a funeral a bit of a lift, a touch of style. One of the handsomest funerals of this year was that of an old farmer who insisted on being buried in his own garden alongside the graves of his dogs.

In Caerphilly there's a bricklayer who makes them his hobby. He got hooked on his mother-in-law's funeral fourteen years ago and now goes whenever he can, whether he knew the corpse or not.

"Sometimes he comes home a bit depressed," says

18

"It leaves me speechless—I've only just had that hand-brake adjusted."

his wife. "But nothing, not even cricket on the telly, his other big love, keeps him here if there's a funeral on."

The amateur mourner himself says "I don't like fussy funerals. I can't stand all the crying. I like the ones in the Order of Buffaloes best. There's always some good, strong singing, and people looking happy."

When that grand old engineer, William Foden, departed at the age of ninety-five a few years back, he rode out on Pride of Edwin, a steam traction engine he built himself in 1916. Marching ahead of the coffin, blaring in blazing scarlet, went the Foden Motor Works championship brass band. Now *there's* a way to go.

You don't get the *racy* funerals of old any more. It's ten years now since Johnny "Scarface" Carter, Sid the Con, Nick the Ape and Freddy the Fly were at a funeral together down Camberwell way.

The deceased was a motor trader whose £6,000 Cadillac crashed in flames near Tower Bridge, and so many of the lads turned out that the cortège stretched for a mile. The best wreath, by general consent, was a four-foot billiard table with six legs of red carnations, a green moss surface, and a set of ivory balls and a cue. Lovely funeral.

They can be happy affairs. I was at Pandit Nehru's funeral along with about half a million others, and that was quite a gay scene, with vendors selling chupattis and pop in the crowd. They watched his body pass and smiled fondly because they do not make our mistake of equating the corpse with the life that was in it. There was no hush. How could there be, when everybody wanted to say goodbye?

The English scoff at the Irish wake, not appreciating that it has nothing to do with dogma or superstition, and very little (apart from a prayer or two) with the corpse, but a great deal to do with sustaining and cheering the living.

I survived one in West Cork earlier this year. Then his friends, as is the pleasant custom, dug the old sailor's grave, but not too deep, for they soon struck another coffin. He barely got below ground, and in the hush a voice said "Jaysus, he hasn't got six inches of free-board." Everybody smiled. Why wouldn't they? They loved him.

Our funerals have become mean, miserable, embarrassing affairs with, at crematoria, as much style as a production line. Dammit, the Chinese hire men to bang gongs and carry crazy floats. We go with a hum of tyres and a hiss of gas. Taped music, an optional extra, is used for solace the way the big jets use it just before landing.

When I go, give me a Basin Street funeral band, Belgian black horses with plumes, a stop at the tap room of The Hermit, and lots of ham. It won't bother me, mate. But it might just take that miserable look off *your* face.

19

HOW CAN YOU PROVE YOU'RE IRISH?

By EAMONN ANDREWS

Almost every second week I meet a returning Englishman at Dublin airport who moves his fishing rod to the other arm so he can get his mouth close to my ear.

"You know, they don't hate the English at all. They couldn't have been nicer. I just don't understand it."

It's all very worrying for the Tourist Board—this creeping malaise of affection that's taking the adventure, the derring do, out of trips to Ireland for stiff-lipped Empire shrinkers.

More than that, it removes one ready made badge of identification for the Irishman himself. All he had to do in the halcyon days was thump the table, raise a red-faced voice and snarl "Damn the English," and it was clear that here now was a true son of Erin.

Worse than that, many of the other sure-fire Celtic ready reckoners are beginning to vanish—the shillelaghs, the pigs in the kitchen, the clay pipes, the hobnail boots.

20

Drink is too expensive to get drunk except at weddings and funerals, and it takes a week's walk in a crowded place to meet anyone even remotely resembling Barry Fitzgerald.

Somebody once defined an Irishman as someone who would step over six naked women to reach a bottle of whiskey. I feel this was something invented by a distiller, unless he meant one of the very few great lovers around the place who felt confident the women would still be there after the whiskey was gone. In fact, if anything, one of the distinguishing marks of the Irishman is that he's not a great lover. He is a furtive lover. First of all, he doesn't want his mother to know that he might even remotely be thinking of loving another woman, and secondly he's inhibited by a long tradition of blackthorn sticks breaking up couples in ditches, of cinemas and churches with men on the right and women on the left, of a terror of having evil thoughts. For generations the politicians have thought that the great emigrant exodus, year after draining year, had got something to do with the economic plight of the country. A more considered but seldom spoken view was that the men wanted to get away to a climate in which they were able to ogle a pretty bird or two without running the risk of being burnt at the stake.

However, it is still quite true to say that he pays lip service and sometimes passionate service to the subject of alcoholic refreshment. A pint of stout or a ball of malt (a glass of whiskey) in the right context can trigger off flights of oratory that would do credit to a Burke or a Grattan or a Bernadette Devlin. Only a few weeks ago, in the *Irish Times*, a quiet and respected architect named Niall Montgomery was driven to dip his pen in vitriol at the rumour that Irish distillers were going to chase the American market by making Irish Whiskey taste more like Scotch Whisky. His letter was headed:

A BALLS OF MALT

"Sir,—The Women of Three Cows and twenty-five counties where an English that the English do not know is the only vernacular, excites the neighbours' pity

"For a drone he's a lot of fun."

with pretensions to thirty-two Erse-talking counties (including Donegal!). Blindness as a national affectation is as much an affectionate tribute to the black-cloaked Profit (stet) that led us into the Promised Land as the Castilian lisp is a tribute to the Habsburgs, but the Irish blindness is no impediment; we look up to our Profits. Madison avenue has shown how even a "genuine article" may be marketable if you can make it look phoney enough; Irish tourism didn't have to be taught that. But the market won't take the one real thing left, Irish whiskey. So the Irish whizz-kids won't make it any more: they'll make Scotch—Scotch, Irish: what's the difference if you can sell it?

But Irish whiskey doesn't belong to a group of manufacturers who have forgotten that they were once distillers—it belongs to the Irish people. The what? They talk a patois of English, they drink an imitation Scotch and they haven't got a damn thing that's not for sale. What would you call them? Erse-liquors?—Yours, etc."

If Irishmen can unite on any one subject they can divide on a million more. No sooner were the English driven out of the twenty-six counties than the natives were at each others throats in bloody warfare. And so it goes on to this day. Although the blood is less the bitterness can be whipped up like a green meringue.

The IRA is splintered into more groups than I know of. The Irish language—a beautiful and musical tongue—which should, at least superficially, unite the Gaels in common affection has created intellectual and patriotic ghettoes. The Irish understood themselves so poorly they tried to force the national tongue by threat and bribe when all they had to do was ban it outright and it would have swept across the plains of Ireland like St. Patrick's fire.

The great Gaelic Athletic Association makes itself ludicrous and almost splits itself in two by banning all "foreign" games. The unbelievable situation is that if a hurling player or a Gaelic football player as much as *looks* at a game of soccer he risks expulsion. It should be funny but it's not; and it will be left to this generation to turn that page of history quickly and quietly.

A classic cheeky illustration of this fatal flaw in our national make up came a few years ago when a committee was set up for the Restoration of Kilmainham Jail—a building of tragic but historic importance. Money was short but offers of help were many. Brendan Behan offered his services as a house painter and was quite serious about it. When the first meeting took place, however, he couldn't resist it.

"Mr. Chairman," he said, as the distinguished and patriotic committee looked on, "may I propose that the first item on the agenda is that we have a split."

By the same token, I remember Spike Milligan telling me how he jumped into a cab in Dublin. As it started to move, the driver said:

"Where to?"

"Kilmainham Jail," said Spike.

"The birds are behaving damned cowardly today!"

22

"Where's that?"

"Stop the cab," yelled Spike, "I wouldn't drive in the same car as a man who didn't know where Kilmainham Jail was."

I asked the same Spike, when I was writing this, how *he* would prove an Irishman.

"Lock him in a room with a bottle of whiskey and a dozen blank sheets of paper. If the paper is filled by the time the whiskey is gone, he's Irish all right."

The old song called for proof in more simple terms.

"Does your mother come from Ireland?"

All you had to do was nod your head at the breath pause and the tenor would sweep you into the club. Nowadays, in fact, a bona fide grandparent or two gives you legal right to claim Irish citizenship.

Recently we had the awe-inspiring spectacle of President Nixon not only landing on the late President Kennedy's other island but claiming Irish forebears—Quakers at that! Democrats are one thing. Republicans another. How it must have shaken some quarters to realise that there was such a thing as an Irish Quaker.

In fact, most people in Britain seem to think that if you're Irish you must automatically be a Roman Catholic. I remember talking to an Irish priest in Glasgow who found his work complicated by this belief, this interchange of terms. He told me of a Polish contingent marching down the street towards the Catholic church where they were to celebrate some feast day or other.

Two Glaswegian shawlies were watching. As the men suddenly wheeled into the church, one turned to the other and said:

"Good gracious! I never knew the Poles were Irish."

All in all, there's no simple proof. I can't give you green litmus paper to carry about with you or test to see if you can play the Uileann pipes. If you cry after two verses of "Galway Bay," you may well be Irish, or simply a sensitive musician. If you fight for lost causes, you're probably close. If you're intolerant of other views than your own, you're probably closer still. But, if you've nothing good to say about the Irish, then you're home and dry. A true Irishman for sure.

"Simpson . . . Eric Simpson, you remember, we were at training school together."

PADDY'S PROGRESS

BILL TIDY follows the hod

"*You're a fool, Dooley . . . the money's over here.*"

"*Sorry boys, the room's taken!*"

"*Dooley! It wasn't you on the steel ball?*"

"*If the police don't start picking on us unfairly pretty soon, we're not going to get into this bloody fight!*"

"*Something's upset Dooley. You don't often see **him** working to rule!*"

"No chance, Dooley. You already owe me two bulldozers and a steamroller!"

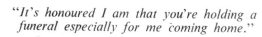

"It's honoured I am that you're holding a funeral especially for me coming home."

M 99 SITE
CLOSED FOR
St. PATRICK'S DAY

"That's what I always say, O'Shaughnessy. If you can't beat 'em . . ."

BALLYKENNA LABOUR EXCHANGE

"Sean, Da says it's nice to have the family all together again!"

"Begorrah, Dooley, welcome back to the only country in the world where a nun buys a round!"

Mutt and Jeff, Laurel and Hardy, Abbott and Costello, and now—Fred and Davey, the latest in a long row of comical exclamation marks. Davey is the vertical stroke, Fred is the dot underneath, a combination well tried in the cause of laughter. These two, however, having cut their milk teeth on the Cambridge Footlights, really came into their own on television, a medium which gave them full scope for their elaborate and costly sight gags. Remember when they parachuted the Dagenham Girl Pipers from the top of the GPO tower, each girl lashed to her instrument and squeezing out the overture to Lohengrin? Transmission time, twenty seconds, and the Accountant not recovered yet.

Both Sides of the Camera

A quartet of telly types by William Hewison

There are telly reporters and telly reporters. The young ones crouch in their combat jackets and deal out chopped bits of sentences breathlessly to the camera; the old one (as here) finds a comfortable corner and extemporises a flow of world-weary chat to no one in particular, a calloused Fleet Streeter who has globe-trotted through twenty-five years of foreign correspondence, a disillusioned cynic who maintains he has seen it all before. His spiel is literate, down-beat, and humane. The bar-room props (again, as here) never vary.

26

"Look, they're all masochists, so don't blame me. They'll sit in front of that camera and confess to three million viewers that they're swindlers, or lesbians, or child-bashers or sodomites. You name it, I can get one. A small-ad in the Personal Column and I tell you, the post-boy arrives buckled at the knees. Why do they do it? God knows. They want to be on the telly, I suppose. Yes, I needle them, I embarrass them, get them weeping or throwing punches. No, it's not unethical, it's 'good television'—and that, as you know, excuses all."

His mum and dad blame it all on the University. "We noticed the change at his first vacation. Nothing said outright, but we knew he was criticising—us, our home, his local friends. Each time he came the gap was wider—he just moved away from his class." Jeremy—Home Counties, Charterhouse, Sheffield University—had discovered The North. "Salford is simply, simply beautiful," he says. "I just adore the configurations of those back-to-backs and the contrapuntal factory chimneys." Top BBC dramatist with fifteen episodes of *Z-Cars* to his credit and a pit family trilogy on the way he remains completely entranced by the working class, but his efforts at flattening his vowels have so far been unsuccessful.

Diary of a Child

by KEITH WATERHOUSE

Monday, 1 March, St. David's Day. Got up. Went to school. Came home. Had fish fingers. Went to bed. Started to count up to a billion but only got up to 7,643 for the reason that, my Father made me stop. He said that if he had to come up to my bedroom once more, that he would strangle me. This man is dangerous.

Tuesday, 2 March, Got up. Had breakfast. Got ticked off by my Father for holding my Breath. People should not get ticked off for holding your breath, for the reason that, it is a free country. Therefore I hate my Father. He thinks he is somebody but he is nobody. Also he have hair coming out of the end of his nose.

Wednesday, 3 March, Ember Day. I am going to get my Father. He has been asking for it and now he is going to get it. Just because I was sucking bread. He go purple and bangs the table. If he was Run Over I would be glad. He look like a Jelly and also is Smelly.

Thursday, 4 March, Moon's first quarter 3.01 a.m. Got up. Went school. Watched telly. Left roller skate on top of stairs, but, it did not work. This only works in comics such as Whizzer and Chips etc., therefore, comics are stupid. They, the people you are trying to get, do not step on the roller skate and go ker-bam-bam-bam-bam-bam-kkkklunk-splat-aaaargh. Instead of this, they just pick up the roller skate and say (This house getting more like a pig-sty every day.). He is Potty and also Grotty.

Friday, 5 March, Today I said I was going to John's house but I did not, I went to the Pet Shop to buy a poisonous snake, but they did not have one. The copperhead, the Rattlesnake, the cobra and the Mamba are among the poisonous snakes to be found in the world. The man in the Pet Shop just laughed and tried to sell me a hamster. I am going to get him after I have got my Father.

Quentin Blake

uerilla

Saturday, 6 March, Sun rises 7.35. I have got an Idea from watching Telly. It is where they were in a certain foreign country and he, the Tall one, invents this special kind of warfare. It comes to pass that this Warfare is something nobody else knows about, therefore he wins it. It is called (long word) warfare. (Long word) warfare is where, they do not fight with guns, tanks, also armoured cars, thus killing them, you fight a person's mind so therefore he will do what they tell them. It begins with the letter P. This I am going to do to my Father.

Sunday, 7 March, 2nd in Lent, 1st day of Operation Stare. Operation Stare is where, you just look at your Father. You do not say anything, you just Look. This was when he was reading the paper, also when he was painting chest of drawers. He did not know I was there until, he saw me. I was just Staring at him. This is Operation Stare. It is (long word) warfare. It did not

work, as he said (If you nothing to do you can tidy up your room). Another example of the poisonous snake is, the sea-snake. He has spots all on his neck. He is Spotty and also Potty.

Monday, 8 March, On this important day I invented the art of making yourself cry. You have to pretend that you have a dog. This could be a Sheep-dog or numerous others, it is called Zebadee. You have to pretend that it runs away in the park and, you come to this swamp and it rescues you and die. After you have gone into the swamp to get it out, the (dog). It dies and you are sorry. This can make you cry, but my Father just say, (Stop snivelling or I will give you something snivel about.).

Tuesday, 9 March, Nothing happened. I am still going to get my Father. I will make him Crack.

Wednesday, 10 March, Birthday of Prince Edward. Today I got my Father to think that I could not move my left arm, also that I could not feel anything in it, it was Dead. I thought this would make him sorry and it did. He went all white and call me Son. He pinch my arm and asked if I could feel it, I replied that (I could not). We had better see Dr. Murray!!! he exclaimed, but just as he was helping me on with my coat to go Dr. Murray, he sticks a pin in my arm accidentally on purpose. This hurt me so I said (Oh). He went all purple and call me Lad.

Thursday, 11 March, Got up. Decided to Lie Low.

Friday, 12 March, Full moon 3.34 a.m. On this day Operation Blink came into being. You just blink your eyes all the time, it drive him Potty. Also, at the same time, you must screw your nose sideways and also make your mouth go down, while you are blinking your eyes. I did this all the time, until my Father Went Out.

Saturday, 13 March, An unlucky day for my Father. On this, the 2nd day of the famous victorious Operation Blink, he take me to see (The Railway Children). I was sick on the bus going, also in the cinema. When we came out, he asked, (Are you feeling

CHILD KIDNAP. KEEP HIM, SAY PARENTS

Larry

29

better now.). I replied that I was, therefore, we went on the bus. I was sick. My Father does not know it, but, I did it on purpose. I have discovered the art of being Sick. It is my secret. I was Sick all over his shoes. The (Railway Children) is a good picture, it better than Rolf Harris. He is Cracking.

Sunday, 14 March, 3rd in Lent. Operation Blink and Operation Sick are still in being. I said I was going to Get him and I have got him. If you keep sniffling, he does not say anything but you can tell he does not like it, this big Vein stands out in his forehead and sort of goes throb-throb. This is Operation Sniffle. This morning I heard him say to Mr. Baker (Are they born like it or what, I don't know what I am going to do with him.). This means that I have won. He knew that I was holding my breath all through lunch time, but he does not say anything, he just Went Out. This also means, that I have won. Today I have started counting up to a billion and have got up to 10,500. I have got to get up to 25,000 before going to bed, or it will mean that I have lost the Battle. He has come back in and, he knows that I am counting up to a billion but, he is just staring at wall and drinking the whisky. It is 3.10 p.m. on Sunday, 14 March, the day of Victory. He has Cracked, and must sign my Terms.

No thank you, I'm trying to give you up

VINCENT MULCHRONE on The Sensuous Woman

I was breaking out my new winceyettes and trying an explora-
tory cough when she staggered into the bedroom with the record player, plugged it
in at her side of the bed, and put on Jacques Loussier swinging Bach.

Keep calm, I thought, and got on with the routine inspection—toe nails, hanky,
glass of water, fags and lighter, and the depressingly small pile of coins where last
night sat a pristine fiver.

"I have been patting myself dry with a towel," she said, "as if I were blotting a
six-hundred-year-old Ming vase." I didn't look up. "Go on," I said.

I am a reasonable man, slow to anger, and anyway I was admiring the "V" I'd
cut in the ingrowing nail on my left big toe.

The Loussier trio were jiving the "Air on a G-String" when there was a "whoosh"
of an aerosol behind me, and the bed-sheets were drenched in cologne.

Humming a sneering snatch of "There's a street in Cairo," I turned to face her
side of the bed, a rare act in itself. She was starkers, pouring a tiny, icy pool of body
lotion between her breasts and massaging it firmly into her thirsty skin.

"It says," she said, "that I have to take my time and luxuriate in my slightly
narcissistic moment."

So *that* was it! It was that blasted newspaper strike. When we couldn't get our
regular paper she got hooked on the *Sun*, which has been serialising a property called
The Sensuous Woman.

It is by a Miss Garrity who, though she claims to be plain, makes up for it with an
enthusiasm which has led her to do it in a four-seater plane, on a deserted stage, in a
swimming pool and even, egad, by moonlight on some unfortunate twelfth green.

And now here she was, buck teeth and all, wreaking her vicarious will in my
bedroom. Even so, it could have been worse. The gay Garrity, who, like many plain
girls, is obviously extremely fit, urges middle-aged couples to perform in patches of
clover, in a park on a rainy day, on a raft in the middle of a lake on a summer night,
and *under* the dining-room table.

(I'm safe there, I thought, in the first flash of comprehension. *We* have a refectory
table, and even the gregarious Garrity couldn't manage it with her kidneys pinioned
on an eight-foot plank.)

Having pin-pointed the enemy I knew what to do next. "Ho, ho," I said,
uncertainly. "So that's your game."

She laughed. As we had spent the evening shuffling unpaid bills, some of them old
enough to have become dear friends, this was an unlooked-for response.

"If you can't laugh together in bed," she declaimed, "the chances are you are
incompatible anyway." Instinctively I managed both to giggle and pluck at the
reef knot in the tickly winceyettes.

"Not you," she snapped. "She's quoting Richard Burton. He says 'I'd rather have
a girl laugh well than try to turn me on with long, silent, soulful looks. If you can
laugh with a woman, everything else falls into place.'" And she laughed again.
But not, I felt, the laugh Mrs. Burton turns on.

Then it all came out. She had been doing a cutting job on *The Sensuous Woman*,
a series which urges forty-year-old housewives to pin a sign above the more or less

marital bed saying "We women were designed to delight, excite and satisfy the male of the species."

I don't know, any more than you do, how you'd explain mummy's little poster to the literate ten-year-old who bursts in at 7 a.m. demanding his porridge.

But if that's what Miss Garrity advises, I can't honestly say that I'm against it. It's her detail that deters.

"If you've got as far as the bedroom with him," she says, "he must have *some* attribute you can admire. Maybe he's got magnetic eyes, or a brawny chest. Well, *say* so."

I tried flexing the general area where my metatarsals sank some years ago, but nothing visible occurred. I didn't attempt the magnetic eyes bit, because whenever I do she mentions that overdue visit to the oculist.

But it's no good feigning a jolly, patronising attitude to the Garritys of this world. If they're going to urge one half of the bed, "Let the flickering light, the softness of the music, the femininity of your scent, the bare freedom of your body, envelop you," it's no answer to lie in the other half sucking a Zube and pretending to be engrossed in A Book at Bedtime.

The thing is—what to *do*? I have toyed with the idea of a counter attack launched by *The Times*. "Sorry, old gel," I'll say, "but this new series in *The Times* says a large whisky to dilate the blood vessels, then straight to beddy-byes."

And, the next night, "It says that a quiet read in bed brings a sense of togetherness unknown on a merely physical level." Or "A steak and kidney pudding, shared, is not so much a meal as a meeting of minds."

It wouldn't work, though. She'd ask to see the cuttings. She'd never believe that The Thunderer could whimper "Leave him alone. There is no higher expression of masculine love than when his head droops and he falls asleep over your cheese soufflé."

Happily, there are chinks in Garrity's own female armour that any man in the hernia belt might penetrate. "One ruse," she says, "is to rise about fifteen minutes

"I know there's not a soul but you to hear me, but I still feel silly shouting 'Mush'."

32

"*Now that's what I call a party.*"

before he does in the morning, so that you can revitalise your face and secretly apply that cheery bit of make-up."

Gotcha, Garrity. Men in your target age-group have kidneys which ensure that *we* are up first, first in with that sneaky cup of tea before she can compose her face, a psychological advantage which has been known to last for twenty-four hours until the next cup.

Garrity goes on a bit, her voice occasionally rising like the barely controlled commands of those BBC radio matrons instructing Form 3A to make like dragons.

"Roll over," she says. "Stretch out. Curl up. Arch your back. Wriggle your toes." A chap *can* concentrate on the Sunday colour supplements with all this going on next door, but it needs nerves of steel.

I got her, though. Garrity, that is. One day she opined: "A hot bath, a gentle massage and a thirty-minute nap after he returns from the office means he'll wake up ready to respond to your advances."

I was heading for the bathroom when I was stopped in my tracks by a sob. "You can't have a bath," she said. "The hot water's gone. I've been washing their rugby kit. I *could* put the immersion heater on . . .

"But then you couldn't have a thirty-minute nap because the Steads are coming round for a drink . . ."

And the massage, I inquired, with a masterful toss of my quiff. She lowered her eyes Japanese style. "Not," she quavered, "while the children are still doing their homework . . ."

We're all right now. The arching and the wriggling has stopped. The lotion has disappeared. On the other hand the regular newspaper has reappeared and last night, out of the corner of one eye, I caught her reading Godfrey Winn. And I thought I caught the sparkle of a tear.

I still bring up the cocoa. I insist. Marriage, I always say, is something you have to work at.

Gilding the Peacock

by WILLIAM HEWISON

I say (and why shouldn't I?) that Vulgarity, thumbing its nose at Art, lies in the prejudices of the beholder. It is not a multi-coloured bauble precisely illustrated in the manual of good taste so that everyone can turn to the page and say, yes, that's it. I reckon it to be something that each of us knocks out for himself, a personal view of what is proper. Or rather, "propah"—a word that can't quite disguise the sneer frozen in behind it. Occasionally we get together with our prejudices and then gang up on the garden gnomes, the Kiss-Me-Quick hats, the pottery geese flying across the suburban wall towards the brass-trimmed telly in the corner, and snigger. Yet the people who have these things have chosen them from a basis of innocent pleasure; in a couple of years' time, when those same geese have passed through shops like GEAR and have alighted on the pages of "House and Garden" as fun-things ripe for SW3—who's going to fix the vulgarity label on them then?

Which brings me to Clothes. (I have been asked, God help me, to tackle Clothes.) These—our dress, what we wear—are even more difficult to pin down. That jazzy tie on the pre-war American may be last year's trendy neck-kipper from Carnaby Street; what was "gaudy" yesterday is "colourful" today; what is judged "eccentric and amusing" by one is thought to be "flamboyant and taste-less" by another. Fashion moves in Its own mysterious way.

Let me start, then, with one of the stock examples of dress vulgarity, one much cited in the men's wear trade press.

Yet this man's dress is completely un-selfconscious; striving after effect is the

last thing he is doing. Vulgarity comes on the scene only when people strive just that bit too hard.

Like this man—loud, extrovert clothes for a loud, extrovert personality.

Yet just as ostentatious (i.e. vulgar) is this man. And I would say that his personalised number-plate showed as much vulgarity as a gardenful of painted gnomes.

And is this man more, or less, v than the one below? There's nothing much to choose between the see-through blouse and the orna encrusted uniform.

And what about Women? Who gets the prize between these two? The first can be seen, I suppose, anywhere on the Costa Brava; the second at any First Night at the theatre. Both of them, when putting together their assemblage, have failed to recognise the point when enough was enough.

As has this one, right from the beginning. She wants to be a teenage dolly-girl, but is twenty years too late.

My own choice would be any mother who puts her two-year-old daughter into a bikini. She may think her child looks "cute"; she may be acting from faint tremors of English puritanism—either way, I claim this is vulgarity. Idiosyncratic? I suppose so. And to indicate just how idiosyncratic I am (and I'm the one who thinks that Nancy Mitford was Non-U for writing about that U/Non-U business—just as I am vulgarly making money out of this feature) here below are one or two items that I feel come on the wrong side of the Vulgarity fence.

One last thought: Is there not something particularly ostentatious about a person who demonstrates his impeccable good taste?

A Short Life, but a Trendy One

By ALAN COREN

Far and few, far and few,
Are the lands where the Trendies live;
Their heads are green, and their hands are blue,
And they went to sea in a sieve.

Old misprint

His birth had been a difficult one. It need not have been, but then trendiness has nothing to do with need, and everything to do with difficulty. It is the hardest thing in the world, as he was to learn, to be impeccably trendy. His parents were rich: his mother might have chosen a private ward and an epidural anaesthetic, and have felt no pain at all; but private wards in major hospitals were not In that year. She might have plumped for natural childbirth and an honest yeoman midwife, because honest yeoman midwives had been very In the year before. But they were

"*We used to bang through about the fiddle player next door, until we learned that he is a quite famous virtuoso.*"

utterly Out now. It was not easy to find a new, swinging, pacesetting method of delivery, but she persevered. Eventually, she had him under a bush. There had been incalculable difficulty in finding a suitable bush in SW3, but grit and neophilia won through.

Soon afterwards, their friends were forced, grudgingly, to agree that death in labour was just about the trendiest way to go, which brought his father enormous consolation.

It was thus left to him alone to tackle the agonising task of naming the baby. It would be almost impossible to cap, say, Auberon Waugh's triumph in naming his child Biafra (even though, time being the capricious thing it is, nobody could now remember why it was that Biafra Waugh had seemed so shatteringly trendy, least of all B. Waugh himself, who wanted to be called Jim and thereby escape the derision of the untrendy tinies around him), and all the super mythological names had gone out soon after all the Victorian names and just before all the marvellous Middle English names: no trendy worth the title would be caught dead announcing the christening of a Frodo or a Gawayne or an Algy. The parents of little Isambard Kingdom Foskett, who lived next door, could now hardly hold their heads up in public, so Out had the nineteenth century become. But his father was a man of dedication and intellect, and after a week or two of prayer and fasting (his yoga was the talk of Eaton Terrace), he hit upon mineralogy. A plume of white smoke went up from his sauna window, and the name was given to *The Times*.

The next headache was choosing a suitable nanny for little Tungsten: Swedish au pairs, trad English greycoated nannies, brawny Australian students, black mammies, had all had their brief day. There had even been talk of women bringing up their own offspring, and it had made a headline or two in the better glossies, but that, too, had faded with the voracious months. Eventually, Tungsten's devoted father hired three

36

"*He hates to delegate.*"

Securicor guards, who brought the little boy up in an armoured van parked at the bottom of the family pelota court, and the neighbours gnashed their teeth at this newsy ingenuity, and went out and rented policemen, but it wasn't the same.

By the age of two, little Tungsten had learned to kill cats with a truncheon, and was immune to tear-gas. He couldn't say anything, but his tight-lipped humourless smile could paralyse a cobra.

So his daddy sent him to an extremely advanced play group; which scorned sandpits and building blocks and climbing frames and other ludicrous archaisms, and by the age of four Tungsten could recite the whole of *The Persecution And Assassination Of Marat As Performed By The Inmates Of The Asylum Of Charenton Under The Direction Of The Marquis De Sade*, and could do passable impressions of Churchill and Pope Pius XII. Nor was his French provincial cooking at all bad.

From there (Eton, Winchester, Holland Park Comprehensive and Borstal all having followed one another into square oblivion) the seven-year-old Tungsten was sent to the New Free School (fees £600 per term), which was run by a group of teenage sociologists presided over by one of England's most respected pushers, where he was taught to express himself. Since education was looked upon as an encroachment on the freedom of the individual, Tungsten was left in a field during the summer and in a shed during the winter, emerging only to give interviews to *New Society* and Desmond Wilcox. As a teaching experiment, it was entirely successful: by

the age of eleven he had constructed a lean-to made of twigs, learned to live off berries and the slower rodents, conquered scurvy, and was bringing up foxes as his own children. All this, without ever having worn shoes or taken a single intelligence test or played cricket or carried a satchel or gone to Hatfield House or eaten mince, or done any other of the awful things that go to make up the nightmare of ordinary youth.

Naturally enough, by the time he reached eighteen he was old enough not to go to university: at least, not in the dreadful square sense. The ludicrously passé prisons of Oxford and Cambridge had now been joined on their scrap heap by the briefly trendy Sussex, Essex, Wessex, Nossex and all the other institutions unthinkingly thrown up by a government of grey, plodding anachronisms, and even the Free Universities and their loose curricula of sniping, looting, sodomy, psychotherapy and other formal disciplines were now the province of the lumpenbourgeoisie, mere training grounds for ICI and the Civil Service. So Tungsten passed a fashionable year or so in Sarawak and Abu Dhabi and Barrow-in-Furness, rounding off his education, before entering upon a career.

His father, meanwhile, broken by bad acid and ever-younger anti-marriages, had died, leaving Tungsten the entire fortune made by his Graphic Design Consultancy Service. Which was just as well, since all the once-trendy careers had been closed by over-use, and no one of taste and inventiveness could be a photographer, or a male model, or a personality, or a tie-

dyer, or a croupier, or a switch-hitting groupie, or a boutiquier any more, and even to think about marrying a princess was to invite derision of an intolerable order. There had been a period, true, when everyone who was anyone had gone for the new craze of butch jobs—navvies, platelayers, sewermen, greengrocers' assistants, and so on—but the trouble with these swinging positions, it rapidly emerged, was that they didn't pay anywhere near enough to maintain a person in the vanguard of trendiness: forty hours down a mine brought in less than the down payment on a pair of Kurt Geiger Gaiters For Him, and the money required to keep the secret places of a riveter smelling of le mistral, which was that season's In-odour, left only small change rattling dismally in the pay-packet.

In fact, as Tungsten rapidly found out, there wasn't even time to work at all if one took life as the serious challenge it was: trendsetting, the thinking-out and the execution, had become a full-time occupation. Sometimes, he wondered whether his father's million would actually be enough.

For example: he married quickly, since marriage was back In, but whereas the vows might once have been sworn, passably trendily, in Brompton Oratory, or Caxton Hall, or Hampstead Registry Office, or,

better, some photogenic village mosque, all these had fallen into common use, along with shipboard ceremonies and the once-trendy jumbo afterdeck. They might have gone for a simple bond forged aboard a Polaris underneath the Arctic cap, had three couples not done so the week before. Instead, Tungsten and his elderly bride (the Youth Scene had long since passed) were forced to wed in a Borneo long-hut, their noses joined with a rat's rib, their wedding breakfast a somewhat sinewy ship's artificer who had been led to believe that his duties stopped at best man. As all the old traditional trendy honeymoon spots like the Marbella Club and the Costa Esmeralda and Acapulco were now full of parvenu trend-followers, Tungsten and his new wife were compelled to seek fresh fields: they found them in Baffin Land, where the sleet came down for a fortnight, and the eskimos fed them on moth soup and raw gull and insisted on sharing their bed, singing all night.

It made William Hickey, but the couple came home covered in wens and tallow-burns, not happy.

Nor could they live in Islington, or Chelsea, or NW1, or Limehouse, nor anywhere else that other people had already discovered, trended up, and filled to the eaves with slavish followers. It was at this point that Tungsten, protected all his life, came to realise how lonely a

"*Thank goodness they didn't find the pot.*"

*"My compliments
to the designer."*

smilby

trendy's existence was doomed to be, out there on the unexplored reaches of experience where no swinging foot had been before. They experimented with many places, and they forked out many thousands; they tried ghettoes and almshouses, they put up a Graeco-Moorish ranchhouse on Hackney Marshes (it sank), they attempted to open Hendon to the cognoscenti, but it failed. At last, they achieved a small success by buying the Woolworth's in Stratford-le-Bow and moving in, and, apart from the odd inconvenience of erstwhile regular customers banging on their living-room windows and demanding cheap lampshades and Smarties, they were happy for a time. But when an interior decorator took up residence in the Co-op across the street and a titled underwriter moved in to the Times Furnishing Co. next door, they had to move on yet again.

It was the same with cars: the farther out one went, the more adventurous one strove to be, the more oystered one's world, the fewer were the options available. Tungsten, unable to accept either the vulgarity of mass production or the squareness of opulence, Tungsten, who sought only uniqueness, found himself at last the owner of a custom-built vintage beach buggy with a blown-through Furoschetti V-16 engine. It threw him out at corners, it exposed him to every extreme of heat, cold and wet, and every time it required an oil-change, thirty technicians flew in first-class from Milan and stayed at the Savoy for a week while they studied his personalised handwritten manual.

His clothes, forged from experimental alloys, woven from exotic grasses, cunningly moulded from aerospace plastics, carried not only the stamp of singularity, but also its price and discomfort: splintered by weird woods, covered in undiagnosable rashes from arcane furs, he suffered, but rarely enjoyed. If his judgment was wrong, he was ridiculed in the trendy purlieus; if it was right, by the next day his styles were being mass-produced and flaunted by millions (at a hundredth of the price), and thereby devalued and Out.

His parties were almost invariably disastrous: once, a trendy could have got by with a token Ghanaian, or a brace of silent Poles, but no longer. In the derelict Wandsworth factory into which Tungsten had now moved (with his wife, her three lovers, their axolotl, and an ominous collection of carnivorous pot-plants), each successive evening was ruined by an increasingly way-out group of invitees: Monday, say, a tribe of pygmies would stand around, staring; Tuesday, the Estonian government-in-exile would get drunk and weep until the small hours; Wednesday was Siamese-twin night; Thursday, there would be an escaped convicts' dance; and so it went on, ever more dire.

He was twenty-six when it all dried up. The money ran out, the sexual variations were beginning to come round again, there were no new drugs under the sun, he had been to all the vilest places of the world, he had pioneered a thousand worthless modes only to see them snatched up and frittered; and when he looked around, he discovered that he had never done anything very well or for very long, and that he had never been very happy, and that the chances were that he never would be.

When they heard the news, his acquaintances (for a trendy's life inevitably precludes friendship) were universally shocked. To have committed suicide was bad enough in itself, but to have done it by taking a bottleful of not just pills, but pills that absolutely anyone might have purchased in the humblest Boots, was utterly, inconceivably, terrible.

It was the most unoriginal thing that any of them had ever heard.

TRENDURBIA

by GRAHAM

"How quaint! The Davenports are giving a wine and cheese party."

"No, honestly, Mrs. Gibson . . . it's extremely comfortable."

". . And this wall, Harris Tweed
. . blue grey Harris Tweed."

"Would my sleeveless Safari suit
in birdseye wool jersey do for a
fondue party? Or shall I wear my
blazer suit in striped silky slub-
weave fabric?"

"A little man up in Birmingham
makes them."

41

Learning to Swoon Again

DRUSILLA BEYFUS
was too young for Thirties style chiffon and champers but eagerly awaits the promised revival. Author, broadcaster, journalist and editor of *Brides* magazine.

The return of romance is rumoured in the media. As a statement I put it on a par with the news, solemnly spelt out in a newspaper the other day that "sex makes a come-back." Romance is always and forever with us.

Suppose, however, that romantic attitudes become not merely popular, but fashionable, promoted and emulated? One of the many consequences would be a search for a new heroine (a reinstated concept), whose lifestyle, appearance, values and relationships perfectly express the new romantic revival. In films, TV series, novels, magazine serials, she might become as much part of the cultural furniture as, whisper it softly, the groupie girl of the groovy, cool, swinging past.

While everyone is scrabbling around for ideas to help build up her identity, I have thoughtfully produced a few clues. The Credo for a girl who goes romantic might be as follows:

I believe in being chaste and chased, and will not apologise for reviving such a corny old pun, as much of my new lifestyle depends on a confident reworking of tried and trusted old themes.

I promise to donate every pair of tights, my see-through blouse and my unisex bathing trunks to the tombola at the forthcoming Danny La Rue Benefit. At all times I shall sit with my legs crossed and not fling them about any old how as if it did not matter. I will do my best to ensure that when such lapses occur it will matter to men. As a founder member of the campaign to help stamp out boring erogenous zones, I am prohibited from giving a graphic description of the chiffon, silken and elasticised mysteries which enshrine my person in place of neuterising tights.

I shall be content to receive one perfect rose, or one perfect jonquil will do, providing that my suitor swears he has kissed it first. This will take my mind off Dorothy Parker's speculation that one perfect rose is just my luck, why not one perfect Cadillac?

Men hoping to win my favours who adopt a casual recreational approach to sex will be dismissed as old fashioned and hung-up on permissiveness. If this does not do the trick I shall cry. Tears, large, lustrous, welling, will never be very far away these days, and when nature fails I will rely on my tortoise-shell and silver tear dispenser. I carry this around with a companion piece, a container of sal volatile for shocks, such as rediscovering that men are beasts and only want One Thing. There is plenty of room in my reticule (in petit-point embroidery) recently emptied of its load of pot, pills and cigars.

I swear to reform my taste in posters on the wall at home. Down will come Che Guevara, Flower Power, psychedelic-pop and Hells Angels and up will go portraits of the giants of modern romance, Tolstoy, Flaubert, Stendhal, the Brontë's for the oldies, and coming up to date with Barbara Cartland, Denise Robins and Erich Segal of Love Story. My collectors pieces will include blow-ups of Dr. George Steiner and John Sparrow, Warden of All Souls, for his poetic defence of passionate love in *The Times* recently.

I need rescuing, but my lovers must possess a background with classically romantic associations. I shall continue to cast myself as a maid of humble station (no change here as this one paid off in the bad old swinging days), and will succumb to men whose infatuation for me will rise above such petty ties as class, and family and country. We shall, in Byron's words, be "all in all to each other." But not before a great deal has gone on before. It will be love at first sight. Time will stand still. Somewhere along the line we shall vote the world well

lost of love. I may thwart him a little to keep him up to the mark. Life will be sad as romance is always sad. Even when it is happy.

As from now I will be turned on by moonlight, nightingales, the picturesque architectural ruins of antiquity in faraway climes, desert islands, sunsets, waves beating against a seashore, "I'll Be With You In Apple Blossom Time" played softly on the ivories. I shall lose my cool forever.

I am pinning my all on a look first popularised in the Victorian sentimental painting "April Love" by Arthur Hughes. Rosebud lips, a flitting blush and a modest stance have taken over from take-me-or-leave-me boldness. My face will be heart-shaped, registering all the notes from submissiveness to compliance, in mulish defiance of Women's Lib.

My make-up has changed. I have consigned my tear-proof, cling-proof, kiss-proof cosmetics in the Come Looking Great range made by Orgasma to the attic (where one day my grandchildren will excitedly discover them beneath mildewing dustsheets), and gone over to the Born to Blush products. I am to look vulnerable, easily bruised, delicate.

Also I am through with all that old-hat honesty about telling the truth when asked if one's beauty is real or out of a box. Long live the new social hypocrisy which permits the use of the protective little white lie. My fringed eyelashes and wayward curls are real, sir. And that should put a stop to the practice in pre-romantic times of his asking to borrow them both.

Will she really happen, this absurd romantic creature? Before dismissing her presence even in fictional form as wildly improbable, consider the lunatic lengths to which the counter movement, social realism has gone. Only yesterday I heard the NASA authorities refer to the wives of the moon shot men as "primary contacts." We may need a shot of April Love.

". . . and another thing—I don't like being taken for granted!"

What have you done since the war, daddy?

1945 Three Europeans, in something less than perfect harmony.

1970 Today they fight side by side against increasing weight, taxes and parking problems.

1945 Sergeant Smith and Feldwebel Schmidt fighting the last battle.

1970 In Nato they stand united, the war to end war having been postponed again.

1945 Ivan Petrov liberates the Czechs from Nazi Occupation.

1970 Ivan Petrov liberates the Czechs from Liberty.

Twenty-five years of progress reviewed by FRITZ BEHRENDT

1945 Private Mitsubashi leaves Singapore for Tokyo.

1970 Mr. Mitsubashi leaves Tokyo for Singapore.

1945 Kostas Chladakis freed from the camp at Dachau.

1970 Kostas Chladakis on his way to the camp at Leros.

Peter was born in 1945.

For him it's just History.

Why I wrote a best-seller

By NICHOLAS TOMALIN

I wrote my book (which is called *The Strange Voyage of Donald Crowhurst*, costs 38s. at your local bookshop, and cries out to be instantly bought by each and every one of you) because it was there. As its subject is the disingenuous mock-modesty of the typical British hero, who says he climbed his mountain, or sailed his sea "because it was there," this is more than paradoxical, it is embarrassing.

However, I always knew I would never write a book unless absolutely forced to do so. No moral compulsion, urge to create, or fury to declare absolutely forced me; so I had to fall back on a deadline, a lot of money, six months off work, and the threat of the sack. The events I had to organise into 90,000 words, Donald Crowhurst's wonderful hoax voyage round the world, and his subsequent tragic death, were fresh and newsworthy. I knew that if I hesitated they would grow stale and uninteresting. Furthermore, I was discovering from the available evidence a story which factually shaped itself into the most beautiful plot I have ever encountered. It was all just too good not to write.

In these circumstances the moment which kills off most books—that unguarded re-read of Chapter One when halfway through Chapter Five—produced its

"There is no news tonight, better just make it 'Strike—Latest.' "

usual feeling of uncontrolled nausea, but by then it was too late. The bulldozer was moving, and I had to race ahead of it.

Most authors declare that the crucial difference between them and journalists is not only that they are more brilliant, imaginative, or perceptive, but they are less lazy. No journalist can write unless in a screaming crisis, ten minutes late for edition time, after fifty cups of black coffee. This is a reasonable observation. I, for one, cannot write unless something slightly more compelling than a belief in my own talent or wisdom is urging me on. It would, perhaps, be better if more journalists were more industrious, and wrote more methodically. It would also be a good thing if more authors were more lazy. This would mean fewer books; I doubt if it would mean fewer good books.

Obviously, writing for non-writing reasons tends to produce hack-work. It also removes the romantic pretentiousness that so easily inflicts writers, particularly when they undertake a solemn long work. Faced with hack-work, or incompetent artyness, I think I prefer hack-work.

For the fifteen frustrated years I was a journalist without a finished book, I often used to ask my fulfilled friends and colleagues how they had done it. It's easy, they would reply. We can all write a good 5,000-word article. All that requires is a flying start and sufficient carbon paper. A book, after all, is only 100,000 words and therefore can be made by writing twenty 5,000-word articles.

I have read many books like this. They fall neatly to bits, like badly glued furniture. For about five years they were called "Anatomy of Something or Other," each organ of the whole being a 5,000-word piece. Nowadays they are called "The Making of Something or Other." And they're always made of 5,000-word pieces.

I see the 5,000-word argument as ridiculous as the argument which says running twenty miles is only sprinting 100 yards 35,200 times in quick succession. The long haul is a separate art. It has a structure, and a nature that is totally different from short sprints. Just because it is a lengthy grind the grim necessity needs to be even more compelling. You have to learn, for a start, to continue writing about something after you have become bored with it. Most books show this; I hope mine doesn't.

One final tip. It helps to have an electric typewriter and a co-author. My electric typewriter was a continual inspiration. A toy that never failed to amuse and instruct. My co-author, Mr. Ron Hall, was also very useful. He in fact re-wrote more or less the entire book. is also extremely competitive. And works by night. The writing of the Donald Crowhurst book therefore became something more of a *race* than a creative endeavour. Each night he would recast my chapters; each

day I would recast his. Breakfasts and dinners, when we were both awake, were unpleasant meals, but otherwise this was an extraordinarily successful working method.

It's very clear to me that the author—whoever he was—who said that nothing concentrates the mind so wonderfully as the threat of execution on the morrow, never wrote a book with Ron Hall as his co-author. In fact, nothing concentrates the mind so wonderfully as the threat of Mr. Hall, who is also your executive editor at the *Sunday Times*, preparing to write another thousand brilliant words before breakfast.

Why I didn't

By ALAN BRIEN

There was a time when I used to feel guilty about not having written a book. It was like being the last boy in the class to smoke, the only bachelor at the dinner party. It got so that I began to wonder whether I was queer—a great, hulking, overgrown, middle-aged journalist afraid to make it with the big boys between hard covers. I would invent all sorts of feeble excuses. My doctor has forbidden me to type anything longer than 3,000 words . . . I just never met the right publisher, I guess . . . I'm half-way through the blurb and I've got this mental block . . . Supposing my mother read it . . . I had this tremendous idea all worked out to the last detail then I discovered Kingsley Amis had already used it . . .

Then I thought one day—what the hell am I apologising for? For not being remaindered in the National Book Sale? For not coming at the bottom of Other Notices? For not reaching an audience that would not support the littlest of little magazines? For not being able to put the cover on the typewriter on Friday afternoon and say "It will be better next week?" For not having to lead deputations to Lord Eccles asking for an extra penny every time somebody turns to my article in the public reading room?

Publishers, like all seducers, pushers, con-men and recruiting sergeants, have a smooth line in sweet talk so long as you say "No." They always try to make you feel embarrassed at not belonging to the club. "Still wasting your vital energy on one-night stands," jeers one. "You're getting too old for cruising after those bits of articles, practising *graffitus interruptus* and pulling out the paper just when the action is getting interesting. Give up being a short-time, twice-a-week hustler. After the hurly-burly of the newspaper office, you need the deep, deep peace of the bookshelves. Believe me, you'll regret going on with these squalid affaires with promiscuous Fleet Street editors. It's time for a secure, lasting, mature relationship with a serious man of letters. I'm asking you to marry me."

The trouble is—he's married already. And not just married, you'll be one of a harem. Like any fortune-hunter in pursuit of an heiress, his interest in the actual body of your work swiftly declines after the contract is signed. If the dowry doesn't come through, you'll find it hard to attract his attention however sexy your dustjacket.

Another publisher operates on the assumption that authorship is a drug. "Come on, baby, kick the kid's stuff. A book, man, it's the main-line, the big, 80,000-word trip. Let's get those colour supplements rolling." But once you're hooked, he knows you'll be an addict, hanging round the trade counters begging for a quick advance on the manuscript.

Yet another specialises in selling the illusion that the book is somehow already finished—all you have to do is type it. "I've sold the serial rights, the paperback rights, the foreign rights, the film rights. We've got it blocked out, down to the last misprint, just waiting for the correct name on the spine." But it's re-typing that gives you the calluses, when you have to work in a part for Peter Fonda, cut out the chapter which will offend the Japanese, and change the old granny into a young black lesbian.

Part of the Mephistophelian mystique of the publisher lies in his ability to make you feel all your objections to authorship are shameful ones. But I know better than anybody what my books would be like. Frankly, I'd rather write them, even, than read them. I'm a short-sprint specialist—up one column, down the next, attaboy, you can't win them all. I like to still remember the first sentence while I'm putting the full-stop to the last. I enjoy seeing what I've written on the streets before I've forgotten it. Nobody expects the Oxford and Cambridge crews to row the Atlantic, or Andorra to launch a rocket to the moon, or Ronnie Corbett to play Coriolanus. So don't force me to write your book, please. If I do my own, I'll call you.

MILES KINGTON

On the Trail of th

I am sent on a mission

My name is Miles Kington, which is my real name, and I was a humorous writer, or journalist, before all this started.

I had heard about their methods before they contacted me. What they did, so everyone said, was to take you out to lunch, fill you with food and drink till your mind-power was sapped and your will was gone, then suggest that you helped them with their cause. You were so far gone that you had to obey. The whole thing sounded like a bad novel, and a bit silly.

All I can say is that it worked perfectly on me. One day last year the editor (we always call him the editor but nobody knows what he really does) took me to a French restaurant in Fleet Street with small tables and large carafes, and an hour later his face loomed into my vision, smiling and saying:

"We want someone to write about the British secret service."

"I know nothing about the secret service," I heard a voice say.

Then you are exactly the sort of person we want to recruit."

Persuasively his voice went on, talking about the absolute wall of silence and hush hush that surrounds intelligence and security in this country. They needed a man, it seemed, who would be prepared to attempt to pierce this wall, using any method necessary, or failing that to report back what the wall looked like. Persuasively his voice carried on, talking now about money, free phone calls, unlimited carbon paper.

"I will volunteer."

"Good," he said. "But you must remember two things. One, you will get no help from us. Two, put yourself in the position of a member of the public who, for good reasons of his own, wants to contact intelligence, but has no idea how to go about it."

"You're not in any kind of trouble, are you?" I asked anxiously.

The editor smiled.

"Your're on your own now," he said.

I set up contacts

Much of British life is controlled by a communications network which deliberately makes it difficult for people to get in touch with each other. It is called the

ecret Service

telephone system. My first step, as a member of the public with no idea how to contact MI5, was to look it up in the phone book. It is not there. Nor is Secret Service or Intelligence Service. There is an organisation called MIL Casual Wear Ltd., which does not admit to supplying raincoats for spying. They put me in touch with a special service called Directory Inquiries.

"I wish to contact the intelligence service," I said.
"Which town, please?"
"London."
"Which street?"
"I do not know."
"Well, what is the name of the organisation?"
"I am not sure. It was called MI5 in the war books I read at school. I cannot reveal which school."
"A moment please . . . there's a chap here trying to contact MI5."

A whispered consultation. I estimate there to have been about four of them. I could not swear to recognise any of them again. A different voice.

"It's the Ministry of Defence you want, sir. I rang Defence."

"Defence? I can tell you absolutely nothing except that I want to contact Intelligence."
"Hold on a moment."
A new voice.
"Commander Hoskins speaking."
"I wish to contact the intelligence service. I cannot tell you anything."
"What is your name, please."
"Kington."
"And what's it all about?"
"That's not fair! I'd rather not say."

During this interval I could hear two public school voices having a long debate in a large echoing room. They may of course have been two army voices and it might have been a small stuffy room with echo device fitted. I could not rule out the possibility that Commander Hoskins was talking to himself in a big cupboard.

"How did you get this number?"

Success! I had them rattled, on the defensive. I pressed home my advantage.

"Your switchboard, sir."
"Ah. Now, the extension you want is 6156."

I phone extension 6156

"Can I help you?"

"I wish to contact the intelligence service."

"Which newspaper do you work for?"

Could my disguise have been pierced so easily and quickly? I thought bitterly. I decided to tell the truth.

"I do not work for a newspaper."

"Then I can't help you, I'm afraid. I deal only with newspapers."

It was more serious than I had even suspected. Commander Hoskins had put me through to the press officer. I confessed my name, magazine and intention.

"Well, look here, it's no good just ringing up. If everyone like you decided to ring up we'd never get anything done at all. The only thing you can do is write a letter to the Foreign Office."

I decided two things instantly. One, I would not play into their hands by writing to the Foreign Office. Two, I would make sure that all interfering bunglers like the press man at Defence were eliminated at a later date.

I build up my cover

"What are you typing tonight?" said my wife as I worked on the transcript.

"I cannot tell you," I told her.

"Give up smoking? Why?"

I make a contact

As the days passed, my new identity took shape. I pretended that I was a staff member of Punch looking for material on the secret service, and in response to this apparently harmless front the information began to flow. I met an ex-naval officer, an ex-army intelligence man, a crypto-socialist, a journalist, a businessman—all of them had previously been masquerading as acquaintances—and they all had things to tell me. Unfortunately, they were all the same two things. One was that it was impossible to get in touch with Intelligence. The other was that there was a building in Curzon Street that had something to do with it. One of these things I knew already.

Then I met a crime reporter on a daily paper. We arranged to talk at 11 a.m. over a glass of Fernet Branca in a pub known only to the national press, who were also there at the time.

"Let me tell you straight off," he said, "that you won't be able to contact intelligence people direct, however hard you try."

I sighed. "And also, I suppose," I said, "that there is a building in Curzon Street."

His knuckles went white.

"All right, I'll tell you all I know. MI5 is security at home. MI6 is intelligence abroad. Special Branch is attached to Scotland Yard and makes the arrests on behalf of MI5, who never appear in public. There is a certain rivalry between the two—sometimes Special Branch arrests people whom MI5 want left alone. By mistake. Special Branch infiltrates subversive organisations. Not long ago, one of these organisations held a meeting which the chairman was unable to attend, and the Special Branch infiltrator took the chair instead. He proposed a motion to blow up the Houses of Parliament and it was seconded by another policeman.

"There is a pub where anarchists and others meet in Holborn, and MI5 and Special Branch take it in turns to bug meetings. One night Special Branch forgot that it was their turn, and it was the night they planned the Greek Embassy escapade."

"This is all good stuff," I said, "but what does it add up to?"

"That you can't really get close to Intelligence," he said sadly. "People only tell you things if it can't be traced back to them, which means if more than fifteen people know already. You won't mention my name, will you?"

I hire a detective

Near Fleet Street there is a small second floor room which houses a private detective agency called Leada. Also empty tea cups, a safe made of Gothic iron, a tall black typist and a small manager who agreed to put a man for a day on to investigating the nature of the

"So much for your 'just order what they're having at the next table and you can't go wrong.' "

secret service, if we supplied him with instructions and money. As I left, I noticed his phone had no number on it.

I go through the files

One afternoon I spent reading newspaper cuttings on the secret service. I cannot name the paper, but I can reveal that I sat at a small desk in a corner wearing an overcoat and broad-brimmed hat which made it very hard to read the cuttings.

I discovered two things. One is that when Intelligence is not pulling off brilliant coups, it is committing the most elementary blunders like not tumbling to George Blake. The other is that the only journalist who really seems to know something about it is Chapman Pincher of the *Daily Express*.

I find out the number of the "Daily Express"

It is 353 8000.

I take the money and instructions to the detective agency

During my second visit I realised I was getting better at the job, because I noticed more significant details. The cassettes of tape on the mantelpiece, for instance. The copy of *Tan* the black typist was reading. (If she was not black at all, she was certainly putting up a good cover.) And a little box high up on the safe with a clandestine label on it. When the manager wasn't looking, I read it and noted it down. It said HIJKL.

Progress so far

(1) Apart from facts already mentioned, I had heard that intelligence is sometimes referred to as Box 500. By whom, I am not sure. I had been told that the Curzon Street building is called Leconfield House. And a source not so far mentioned had assured me that the head of MI5 is called . . .

Head of MI5

. . . Sir Martin Furnival Jones. This is borne out indirectly by *Who's Who*, who can suggest very little cause for his knighthood.

Progress so far

I had begun to get nervous in crowds and to wear an overcoat about the house.

I visit Leconfield House

"I am a journalist and I want to know what goes on here."

"There's a journalist with me wants to know what goes on here," said the commissionaire discreetly into his phone.

A man appeared and told me at some length that

nothing went on there, that I would have to talk to the Ministry of Defence to find out about all the things that went on there and that *they* wouldn't tell me. He was a man I would find hard to remember again; in fact, I glanced at him several times during the conversation without recognising him.

I collect the detective's report

The report concluded that it was almost impossible to contact MI5 or MI6 but mercifully made no reference to Curzon Street. It reported that:
—the head of Special Branch is F. G. Smith, whose extension at New Scotland Yard is 3436.
—the Army Intelligence Corps has an HQ at Ashford, Kent, for spying and counter-espionage.
—the head of it is Mr. John McKenzie.

—there is a Mr. Roy in Room 308A at the Home Office who claims to be in constant touch with MI5.
—his equivalent at the Ministry of Defence is in Room 4107 is named as "Mayor Davis." (I suspect this is a misprint for Major Davis.)
—security measures have recently been stepped up to prevent calls from cranks.
—this may or may not refer to me.

During my last visit to the agency I found myself idly studying a window opposite and working out how I would escape from it and climb down the front of the building. I suddenly realised that the job was beginning to prey on me.

"*The original is in the British Museum.*"

52

AFTER GÉRICAULT

"I dread to think what the hotel will be like."

I find a memo on my desk from myself

It said: "Try to get through to Chapman Pincher."
Security at the *Daily Express* was obviously lax because
a minute later I found myself talking to Chapman
Pincher. Having persuaded him that I was not using
him as an easy source—that, in fact, he was part of my
material—I was given some very useful advice. Passing
over the impossibility of ever contacting intelligence
services, unless they come to see you for their own
purposes, we come to this passage.

"Intelligence people keep themselves secret because
their faces and identities must never be known. If you
once get your picture in the paper you are no use. Heads
of the services are usually kept secret, simply to preserve
the privacy of their home and social life. It is possible to
build up contacts, as I have done, but they are always
changing—they go abroad, they get promoted too high,
they retire or die, they just clam up.

"The main thing to remember about intelligence
and security is that it is always a balance of probabili-
ties. One side has a success, the other side does something to make it look as if it wasn't a success. You can

never be sure if your good contact isn't also a good
contact for somebody else. After ten years you can call
a case closed and say, 'Well, we won *that* one anyway—
I think.' They never really know.

"Actually, you couldn't do much better than get my
new novel on the setup, which sets the picture pretty
well."

Or, presumably, so he thinks.

Conclusion

It is impossible to contact the secret service directly,
unless you really have got trouble, in which case call
the police or Mr. Roy. There is an ugly building in
Curzon Street called Leconfield House. Otherwise
there is no way of knowing what my information adds
up to.

Finally, if anyone wants to contact me, I'm afraid it
will be useless. I shall be sitting at my desk in the office
reading Chapman Pincher's novel with strict instructions not to put calls through. At least, I shall be as soon
as my researches have disclosed what the name of the
novel is.

53

"Cyril Connolly said the book was the obscene ramblings of a decadent, perverted lunatic and all we get from you is 'I like it! I like it!'"

"I still treasure his first book, it is always at hand, a volume which has helped me as a writer more than I can say."

THE LIT CRIT BIT

by
DICKINSON

"Giles, one can't throw him out. He swears he's the book critic of the Illustrated Carpenter and Builder."

"Here's your big chance, lad. Latest edition of Britannica. Two hundred words by nine tomorrow morning. OK?"

"A tragic mistake. He was sent his own novel to review and he panned it."

In Praise of
MUZAK
by ANDRÉ PREVIN

The first of a new series, in which distinguished

figures take up hopeless causes.

Sometime leading jazz pianist, now Principal Conductor and Musical Director of the London Symphony Orchestra, André Previn is an American composer and conductor whose film scores have won him a string of Academy Awards.

I like to think my musical tastes are catholic. Given the right time and place, I love the Missa Solemnis, Strauss Waltzes, Duke Ellington, Josquin des Pres, the latest tape concoction for soprano, airplane motor, bass flute and telephone, Rachmaninov, Blossom Dearie, the Beatles, Percy Grainger—anything. Come to think of it, I do have one blind spot: Hawaiian music, which affects me violently and fills me with hatred. But all those other categories of music are dear to me, and I have seen articles, essays and whole volumes of praise for all of them. However, there is one kind of music which has been shamefully neglected by the pundits, from Neville Cardus to Tony Palmer—and that is muzak.

Muzak is a phenomenon of our time. Music to be heard but not listened to. This particular stepchild of St. Cecilia doesn't need the "time or place" of more sophisticated forms of music. No snobbish Festival Hall, no august university surroundings, no gleaming stereo equipment—no, thanks, this is one of the crowd, friendly, ubiquitious, always present but shyly in the background, ready to soothe, placate, a murmuring placebo, the adult's dummy, sucked on by all ears in lifts, airplanes, doctors' waiting-rooms, department stores, railroad stations, and other human meeting grounds where otherwise we would be afflicted by the most feared of all situations —silence. Silence, as every denizen of our century knows, must be avoided. It would allow one to think, thinking might lead to conclusions, and before you know it, the populace might all be booking passages to the moon.

But to praise muzak only for its tranquillising qualities would be like praising the British railway system only for its food. No, no, as a professional musician I find many detailed aspects which elicit my attention and command my admiration. First off, there is the total mystery of who the contributing artists are. Who writes those arrangements? What musicians actually play them? Where are they recorded? Obviously, muzak is a huge industry, probably earning annual millions; yet I have never, in all my travels, encountered any single musician who has admitted to participating in any of the stages of making muzak music.

I visualise modern-day press gangs invading the pubs near Abbey Road or Kingsway or Denham and carrying off screaming, luckless clarinet players, doomed to recording sessions of "Gems from *The Pink Lady*" in some dank cul-de-sac. Perhaps, once there, masks are distributed, thus ensuring anonymity forever and giving the recording sessions an Ensor-like quality of horrifying humour. Whatever the circumstances may be, the fact remains that muzak must regularly employ thousands of musicians every year. I suppose one could argue that the money is ill-gotten, but we

have learned to look upon the pianist in the Storyville whorehouse with good nature and even admiration, so perhaps one day there will be a Kirk Douglas movie about the struggling muzak trombonist.

So much for the economic advantages of muzak; now let's examine the artistic gains. One cannot forget that the repertoire emanating from those speakers cunningly hidden behind the imitation Utrillo in the dentist's waiting room fills a gap which otherwise would be left empty forever. Of the many sub-divisions in this category, let's begin with classical music. Where else would you hear representative portions of the oeuvres of Chaminade, Paul Lincke, Cyril Scott or Charles Wakefield Cadman? Granted, the orchestrations, tailor-made for muzak, make it difficult not to fall into a catatonic state after, say, two and a half measures; one of the ukases handed the arrangers must be not to do anything noticeably loud or soft, fast or slow —just to keep a steady paralytic tempo and a medium dynamic, akin to audible Nembutal.

But to those hardy musicologists able to stave off the sandman, the rewards are myriad. What a cornucopia of lost treasures: *Scarf Dance*, *To A Wild Rose*, *Lotus Land*, *The Merry Farmer*, *Glow Worm*, *The Satin Slippers* all come tumbling out in rich profusion. And the programming is extremely clever; not too much of that heavy stuff in a row. No indeed, with their fingers on the pulse of the people, the computers know that a surfeit of those aforementioned classics could lead to impatience.

On to gayer fields: musical comedy. Only token respect is paid to Rodgers and Hammerstein, Lerner and Loewe and their ilk, but the real emphasis again lies in the thrill of rediscovering the irresistable medleys from *Sunny River*, *Kelly*, *Portofino*, *Twang*, *Buttrio Square*, *What's Up*, as well as the student work of Friml, Romberg and Herbert Stothart. Shows which close on Broadway after a forced run of three nights might have to burn the scenery, but the scores are snapped up by the eagle-eyed scouts from muzak, eager to solidify their service to musicology by continuing their scholarly perusal of the History of Flop Musicals. Only the Durant's monumental volumes of the history of civilisation can rival such unflagging devotion to a cause.

Then there is the quality of the performances. They are really damned good. Everybody plays immaculately in tune and the ensemble is generally accurate. These instrumentalists are professionals all, obviously working under assumed names and banking in Switzerland. Only the most expert players could perform so consistently at the same level of dynamics, so relentlessly in a moderate tempo, and so smoothly without ever accentuating a single note or phrase. My profession is by nature peripatetic and I have had to stay in hotels all over the world. Thus I have been witness to musical aggregations renowed for their ability to sleepwalk through their repertoire. Collectors of such groups treasure memories of the Palm Court of the Palace Hotel in San Francisco, the Plaza in New York, the Savoy in London, or the Danieli in Venice, but for sheet perfection in rendering everything from Khatchaturian's *Sabre Dance* to *Indian Love Call* in the same soporific state, the muzak orchestras win hands down. In an Aquacade, the clowns taking those ungainly falls off the high diving board are probably the best divers and swimmers of the lot. By the same rule, the instrumentalists in muzak must be geniuses.

So hats off, gentlemen, in praise of muzak; purveyors of forgotten music, gold mine for musicians, enemy of silence, the undiscovered heroes of Pop culture, the perfect merchants of mediocrity, the only audible plastic in the world.

HARGREAVES

"It's no bloody use now—the beans have gone cold."

A Land Flowing with Yoghurt and Carrot Juice

By ALAN WHICKER

Anyone can be beautiful and loved: it's just a question of applying something, take a course, buying a pot, denying yourself—or being operated on, slightly. So say the Archpriests of the religion of beauty, which women spend £100,000,000 a year to practise. To keep up in the Face Race, the average woman in her lifetime also spends four years fourteen weeks and six days in front of her mirror, making-up. It certainly feels that way when you're waiting downstairs.

Men—apart from the fringe fringe—seem unprepared to do much, though still pay-out a crafty £8,000,000 a year; would you believe—*guy*lashes!

By the end of this decade Americans will have spent £4,000,000,000 to make themselves a little lovelier each day—or maybe, to buy a little hope. In view of all this I went to Texas (of course) to observe a species in The Greenhouse, that ultimate purpose-built fat farm which cost a million pounds to contrive and is quite improbable. It stands, a perfumed palace outside Arlington, bathed in the soft glow of money and dedicated to the sale of dreams, the expectation of beauty.

Women of a certain age (and some younger) queue to pay from £50 to £110 a *day* for rejuvenation. Some stay months. The ageing and wrinkled, the plump and bored surrender dollars and dignity in exchange for solace and repair, for the dream of growing younger, fairer, sexier . . . while outside in the harsh sunlight, gardeners symbolically dye dry Texas grass green.

In Britain where we at least let grass decide its own colour, narcissism is also in—observe the march of fully booked Health Farms. Prices may be less extreme but you can still lose, along with avoirdupois, some ninety guineas a week.

A Health Farm means paying a lot of money *not* to do something. At the end of the week you get a breath-taking bill for what you could easily have done at home for nothing if you had the strength of character, which you haven't—so pay up and look small.

I was introduced to an early version fifteen years ago,

57

*"You never tell me
I'm lovely anymore . . ."*

surrendering to its rigours for a radio programme, and later for *Panorama*. Afterwards a number of patients, affronted by evident truths and being filmed Before instead of After, complained to the BBC. They did not notice I was hooked on the good sense of it all.

Such instant affront is one of the problems of television: nobody wants an accurate image of anything near to home; the preferred picture is blurred, gently distorted, romanticised, approving.

I filmed a *Whicker's World* programme on a most enjoyable cruise. Afterwards the shipping line spokesman said ruefully: "It was an honest programme, all right. The only trouble was, it was *too* honest." That's the way it goes, tellywise.

At this Surrey health hydro a few were ill but the majority were, quite reasonably, carboholics resisting the temptation, alcoholics drying-out, executives escaping the telephone: "My Chairman goes to the South of France and puts on a stone. I come here and lose one. He feels guilty; I feel great."

Health farms vary from earnest nature cure centres catering for those with little faith in orthodox medicine to stately but antiseptic Victorian mansions where society matrons hold back the years and Show Biz straightens its elbow and resists the sweet smell of excess.

If you are *not* sick there's no doubt one of the cheerier hydros, full of jolly folk expensively repenting excess, is more agreeable than those chintzy halls where arthritic old ladies knit by the fireside, each a silent reproach to the healthy but weak-willed who just want to lose a few pounds, regardless.

Voluntarily incarcerated in one of the serious establishments, I was watching a television play one night amid an enthralled group in dressing gowns; just getting to the exciting bit when a young man in the

statutory white Kildare-coat strode in and switched the set off in mid-sentence. I leapt up in outrage.

"Ten o'clock," he said, reproachfully. "Time for bed." I was about to dash him to the ground when it came to me this was what we were paying for: a return to the secure days of Nanny-knows-best.

Once you've accepted such discipline there's a certain relief in surrendering to white-coated father-figures who know what's good for you, in having your days planned down to the last orange juice. There's the grin-and-bear-it Dunkirk spirit of the carrot cocktail bar where you swop losses; the lazy pastoral pleasures of a country estate; the satisfaction of growing, if not a little lovelier, at least a little *smaller* each day.

I remember another Correspondent in Ismailia during the riotous days when the Egyptians put a match to Shepherds, the late Bernard Wicksteed who wrote Tubby Hubby columns for the *Daily Express*; when he left his first health farm, he told me, he was "walking a foot off the ground." There surely is new delight in old suits that not only fasten without strain, but hang loose.

We are today in the middle of an expansionist trend, with 10 million men and 12 million women overweight. Insurance companies say a man of 45 who is 25 lb. above his proper weight lowers his expectation of life by 20 per cent. Put another way, he'll die at 60 when he might have reached 80 . . . We spend £25 million a year on slimming foods which taste like crushed cardboard, lotions, massage equipment, pills; but you lose it best by practising one simple exercise, performed sitting down—and don't think it's easy. You shake the head from side to side when offered a fattening plateful.

A sensible girl I took out in New York refused her apple pie à la mode with the telling comment: "A moment on the lips, a lifetime on the hips."

*"Like in the old song, Mr. Frobisher—
eat, drink and be merry . . ."*

"You'd better get washed and changed. They're having company."

Americans, needless to say, have the ultimate diet: the Zero-Calorie, which means you just don't eat. As you might expect, it works.

Elaine Johnson, a 35-year-old housewife, was almost 20 stone and so fat she couldn't cross her legs, or sit without breaking the chair. She started the diet after getting wedged in a cafeteria doorway, a significant time to face facts. In four months she lost eight stone. At the same California hospital Bert Goldner weighed 425 lb.—almost 4 cwt.—and was so spherical he couldn't sit or lie without fainting from lack of oxygen. He had to sleep standing up or kneeling. During a nap he once toppled over and broke his leg.

You see how helpful it is—*reading* about diets. I feel thinner already.

The form at a fat farm is a Sunday arrival with a pseudo-medical test that evening: blood pressure, heart beats, weight and the old Army how-do-you-feel routine. The usual treatment is a complete fast, by which they mean three oranges a day. Should you be determined to surrender the whole hog, three glasses of hot water each day, with a slice of lemon to take the taste away.

Mornings are filled with mild action: osteopathy,

ultra-sonic therapy, infra-red and radiant heat, saunas, steam and sitz baths, various combinations of sweat-inducing bakery: mud, wax, cabinet, peat, blanket baths.

Best of all, massage and manipulation which comes in all possible forms, from pleasurably painful to Wake up, Sir. As I always say, it's nice to be kneaded; but a health farm's asexual: all slap, no tickle.

Looming ominously behind such agreeable time-fillers: enemas and colonic irrigations. Nature cure enthusiasts explain that in decoking the engine, waste poisons must be swept away for a fresh, empty start—and that's the way they gotta go. This may be medically sound but true or false, it's not much fun.

Various spin-off activities, or non-activities, seem more therapeutic: complete rest (or stultifying boredom); non-availability of demoralising distractions, like pleasure; the spiritually up-lifting sensation of being above temptation, per force.

I derived additional benefit by giving up smoking 50 a day, on the assumption that if I had to be unhappy anyway, I might as well be utterly miserable. On a fast, mouth coated with dark fur, cigarettes are resistible and the whole system so outraged that one further

deprivation goes unnoticed. I commend this ploy to the addicted.

I also—giant stride for one man—cleaned my car. This beneficial, constructive exercise can occupy an afternoon or two. Unfortunately I have had no time for health farms during the past five years, so the car now needs another visit even more than I do.

The Metropole at Brighton recently opened the largest health hydro in Europe. I attended its inaugural week-end; a cheery group drinking mimosas on a private pullman train, inaugural lunch, a week-end of fun and slimming treatment. Without any effort, I put on five pounds.

This hydro may now close, the management realising what anyone as weak-willed as I could have told them before we left Victoria: serious dieting demands monastic seclusion—several thousand acres and long country lanes between you and the nearest steak house. At the Metropole the Other World was down there in the dining-room every night, visibly stuffing, while outside on the promenade, the ice cream bars beckoned . . .

Nature cure is not merely an expensive folly; ignoring its unwordly cancer-cure fringe, the theory seems eminently reasonable: rest, restraint, simple food. The advantage of a farm's outrageous expense is that one may be stunned, upon release, into sensible eating. Write off those who triumphantly smuggle scrummy tuck into bedrooms, or creep off on afternoon dainty-tea crawls; their weighty problems are here to stay.

The ideal fortnight, down on the farm, is ten days' fast (during which you lose a stone) and four days' gentle return, via yoghurt, to salads and plain food; this puts four pounds back into that shrunken stomach. The more flab you take, the more you leave behind; heavy drinkers and the very fat see it drop away, revealing long-lost toes.

Mealtime behaviour after release depends upon your good sense and the impact of the bill. Most edge slowly back to the weight they took with them; sterner souls change their life pattern, better and smaller people for ever.

All right—so I got the car cleaned.

"Well, it was the 'in' place last year."

SUNNY STORIES

So much of the world's great literature is spoiled by unhappy endings. Life would be far merrier if . . . .

From PARADISE TEMPORARILY MISPLACED, Book XII
by John Milton

. . . . . High in Front advanc't
The brandisht Sword of God before them blaz'd
Fierce as a Comet. "It is goode of Him
To turne out in this filthie Night to showe us
Home," said *Eve*, but *Adam* merely shrugged:
"Hee has had time to thinke, and now can see
Clear as th'Abbyssian Cougar when he huntes
At Afric dawn the Potto on the Plaine,
That Sexe is normal, natural, helthie, goode,
And that Himselfe the Apple first did plant
And therefor has Himselfe aloan to blame."
At this, softe Thunder roll'd across the skye,
Apologising; and the Gates did ope
For our proud Parents in their figgy State.
They hand in hand with sinuous steps and slow
Back into *Paradise* took thir lusty way.

From THE SPY WHO STAYED IN WHERE IT'S WARM
by John le Carre

"Drive at thirty kilometres," the man said. His voice was taut, frightened, but with a merry Balkan ring. "I'll tell you the way. When you reach the place, you must get out and run to the wall. The searchlight will be shining at the point you must climb." Leamus was touched by the man's kindness, felt snug and happy as they cruised through picturesque East Berlin in the smooth-running Wartburg. "Golly," he said, "it does seem a shame to be off so soon. I can't help admiring, for instance, the way people's architects have striven towards harmonious solutions to the problems linked with requirements of most modern city, using only the most up-to-date tools. I wish I had taken more snaps of the Karl Marx Allee. Why, when I was a boy, 20,743 Berliners were still in cellars confined by the capitalist social order." The soldier smiled wistfully. "Mr. Leamus," he said, "I am so happy to see you have enjoyed your visit to the Democratic Republic. I myself used to suffer. Today, I have a place in the State wool and buttons store overlooking the Friedrichstrasse. We could use a man with your eye." Leamus needed to think hard. "Do you know," he said at last, "I think I'd like that, comrade. I'd like that very much."

Schubert's Symphony No. 8 in B minor

From HAMLET, Act v, Scene ii
by Wm Shakespeare

Queen No, no, the drink the drink—O my dear Hamlet! (*Falls*)
Hamlet O villainy! Is't poisoned?
Queen No (*Gets up*)
Hamlet But yet Laertes shall be better served
     If yet deserts shall be more mete than sweet! (*Stabs Laertes*)
Laertes Sweet Heav'n, I'm slain! (*Falls*)
King That dagger is but rubber, honest Prince! (*Laertes recovers*)
     Take this, the steel, and thus despatch our sorrow!
Laertes (*Snatches dagger*) Die, Hamlet!
Hamlet O naughty Death, I run to thee and—Oy!
     This blade has e'en retracted in its hilt!
     It is a player's weapon, just a toy
     To prick the groundlings' laughter from their ribs!
     But, Claudius, since thy will was adamant,
     Then let my iron strike! (*King falls*)
(*Enter Ophelia, dripping*)
Hamlet O maid, I have my uncle just despatched!
King (*Recovers*) Not so, my lord! My trusty iron vest
     Hath once more stood between me and my God!
Horatio What's this? Is no one dead?
(*Examinent omnes*)
First Gravedigger Pah!
Second Gravedigger Faugh!

(*Exeunt*)

From THE LADY OF SHALOTT
by Alfred, Lord Tennyson

Under tower and balcony,
Past the cheering gallery,
A gleaming shape she hurtled by,
Bright red between the houses high,
    Revving into Camelot.
Out upon the wharfs they burst
To see which powerboat had come first,
And past the post the captain nursed
    The Lady of Shalott.

The editor of the Morning Post
Gave him the cheque, then drank a toast
To the powerboat with the most
And watched the slender vessel coast
    With the tide to Camelot:
But the editor sighed a little sigh;
He said, "Our funds are running dry;
I think that we may be sued by
    The Lady of Shalott."

"*This is the wall, Foster. We'd like you to knock up some sort of apt and symbolic mural—you know the sort of thing—The Chairman and Board presiding over the Twin Spirits of Art and Industry as they rise from the Waters of Diligence to reap the rich harvest of Prosperity while the Three Muses, Faith, Hope and Charity flanked by Enterprise and Initiative, bless the Corporation and encourage the shareholders.*"

"The junta idea didn't work out."

Violence is Nice

By JOHN WELLS

How can we learn to live with violence in 1971? Some tastes take time to acquire. Sophisticated pleasures, like eating oysters out of *The Times*, take longer getting used to. So it is with violence, particularly if you are on the receiving end of it. For many people, just completing perhaps a tower of pennies for the RSPCA when it is swept off the bar by a drunken Women's Liberationist, or lovingly adding the final gloss to their 1913 Sunbeam Smokeless, only to see it overturned by enthusiastic students bent on burning Barclays Bank, violence must often seem irritating. But now, with the publication in this country of Dr. Bipsi Wollbaum-Goebbels' *Pig-dog!*, there is at least a chance that such people may be persuaded to be more tolerant towards violence in all its many forms in the coming year.

Dr. Goebbels' argument is based on the premise that nature itself is violent, and that to deny violence is to deny nature itself.

"How great a stress," she writes, "the Western Bourgeois Capitalist lays upon Order. For him it must be to wake up each morning in the same bed, Hello, Good Morning to the same woman. How different it is for our own Mao Tse Tung! Then Crack Crack with the spoon on the same cooked egg, out through the same front door past the same oh-so-neatly cut grass lawn, and into the railway station to catch the same electric train. Can we imagine Mao Tse Tung in such a context? This same Order reflects itself in the regularity of his enfeebled sexual assaults upon his secretary, and in the equal regularity of his bashful apologies. How Mao Tse Tung would laugh also at the pedestrians proceeding in an oh-so-orderly fashion along the pavements and not up the middle of the streets, where the dull-minded conformists of the internal combustion engine proceed in an equally ordered manner up and down the road in oh-so-well-disciplined columns.

"It is for this reason that the Western Bourgeois Capitalist is surprised, walking along his clean, mathematically patterned pavement, when the heroic political activist leaps up from behind a dozing Traffic Warden—Gestapo-style guardians of this pathetic orderliness—and hits the Capitalist Thunk on his bowler hat with a paving stone. The Capitalist is confused: such an event is not expected in his oh-so-cosy system: his eyes draw together for consolation and Krump he collapses."

Dr. Goebbels' thesis is that the Capitalist should welcome this intrusion of life into his dead world: certainly he has no cause for complaint or self-pity.

"Does the volcano cry 'Alas, I have a splitting headache' when the inexorable flood of molten lava bursts upwards and explodes the mountain top? Why then the businessman in his bowler hat? Does the egg shell

complain when the little chick cracks it up the middle? Does the tortoise raise any objection when the marauding gorilla cracks *its* shell on a rock and eats it? No, they do not. And why for not? Because each humbly accepts his role in a dynamic and swiftly exploding universe where peaceful order is a symptom only of death. To find such humility in the businessman we seek in vain.

In a chapter specifically addressed to the victim of political or random violence, Dr. Goebbels urges the elderly members of racial minorities and so-called innocent bystanders to muse on these natural images. "As the lead-filled stick bites into the scalp and begins to create the fascinating map of tiny bifurcating fissures in the skull, concentrate on the volcano, the egg-shell, the humble tortoise. Similarly when the steel-tipped boot lifts with breathtaking impact into the soft organs, gristle and fragile bone-structures. In this way, often with a flash of enlightenment, the individual sees his place in the universe, bowing before the dark forces of historical inevitability."

In answer to critics of violence in the abstract who argue that it can achieve little but a return to authoritarian extremism, Dr. Goebbels winds up with an exhilarating chapter in its defence on a purely personal level. "So many years drag by without crisis or excitement in our personal lives. Cotton-wool-wrapped we creep from womb to tomb. Violence at last offers a way of making yourself felt. Perhaps of making yourself black and blue all over. Make this a year of serious involvement. If you see a fight, a riot, a violent demonstration, an instance of police brutality, rush into it, immerse yourself in the creative process. Exult as the fingers are thrust up your nostrils, feel a deep satisfaction as your head is wrenched backwards. Hooray! What a privilege to be alive, participating in a natural phenomenon! O what fun, says the philosopher, it is to be doing what comes naturally. And when you have the hang of it, why not start inflicting a little grievous bodily harm for yourself? Surprise your friends! You will be exhilarated as never before as you see them becoming red in tooth and claw."

It is an exciting prospect for 1971. As Mao himself has said, if you can't beat them, kick them.

". . . perhaps a little light exercise?"

What the eye doesn't see...

. . . . Everybody grieves over.
Including Michael Parkinson.

Producers are people who stand behind a camera and get a performer to do what they themselves couldn't do in front of it. Generally speaking in television they are underpaid, overworked and often buckle under the stress. I knew one producer who sat in his office all day firing an air pistol at a picture on the wall and another who slept in his office and kept a pot of marmalade and a loaf of sliced bread in a filing cabinet marked "Budgets."

I could tell some funny tales about producers and directors (funny peculiar that is) and I am going to. I speak from a wealth of experience and a fund of knowledge because although nowadays I spend all my time in front of a camera there was a time, and not too long ago, when I too was a producer. The first producer I ever met sat in his office watching a group doing a number on a local programme he was producing. After a while he said "They'll never make it," and switched off the set. It was the first time I had seen the Beatles. It was the same producer who revealed his ignorance of sport by hiring a performer who made his debut with Lew Hoad and concluded the interview with the words "Thank you Rod Laver." Yet he was a good producer, one of the best I ever worked with. It was just that occasionally the strain got the better of his judgment.

When you first enter television you are persuaded to the point of view that producers are special people blessed with a god-like infallibility. They have the biggest offices, the prettiest secretaries and four volumes of *Spotlight*. After a while you realise they are just simple human beings, like yourself, trying to do an impossible job. Their doubts and uncertainties are often apparent the first time they call a group together to discuss a new programme. Then they enter the room, stilling the conversation with their presence. They sit at the head of the table, bring out a huge folder marked

65

"New Programme," and spread the contents in front of them. The assembly awaits the words that will decide their labours in the coming months, eagerly anticipates the explanation of the philosophy of the programme. The producer says: "We've got this half hour slot five nights a week. God knows how we fill it."

The fact is that producers are sleight of hand merchants, experts at running their fingers over a half baked idea and producing a passable item for television. Everything is stacked against them. They never have the money, invariably the performer thinks the show stinks and the researchers will write essays instead of dig for information. And yet somehow the show goes on and miraculously someone sitting in Accrington is mildly amused by it. I am of course talking about those producers who are responsible for the current affairs side of television and not those strange creatures who produce drama and the like and wear coats with velvet collars and don't bite their nails.

When I was a producer myself I had a healthy contempt for performers. I began to change my mind about the time I first started appearing on television. I had been working hard for about a year on a new programme when it was suggested that I might go to Turkey for a few days to do a bit of company business, but mainly to relax and enjoy myself. I had just settled nicely into the Istanbul Hilton when I received a cable asking me to go to Cyprus where the locals were having a go at one another. I did so and having spent a torrid few days on the island filming a civil war, was just about to get back to my room at the Istanbul Hilton when I received a further cable requesting me to go to Zanzibar, which was having a revolution. I flew into that strife-torn island, as they say, only to be arrested on the spot and locked up in the bar of an hotel. I spent a boozy, but none the less frightening two or three days in this situation before being evacuated by the Royal Navy, but not until our captors had driven us twice round the cemetery for a laugh. I arrived back in England feeling like I had undergone a major operation only to be whisked into a television studio to be interviewed about the situation in Zanzibar. After the interview I saw the producer. "That was great," he said. "From now on consider yourself a performer. By the way, old man, how was the holiday?"

"One civil war and one revolution. But the weather was nice, Mustn't grumble," I said.

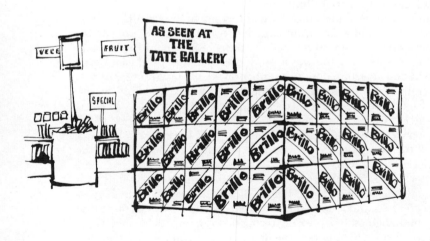

"Hello! We can't be far from civilisation."

It was then that I started to get the performer's eye view of the producer, to see him as a heartless and unscrupulous manipulator of his fellow men. I have mellowed a bit now but there was a time when I preferred our relationship to be an abrasive one. Occasionally my attitude of marked superiority in most things would be rewarded. There was one glorious moment with a particularly pompous producer that I shall treasure for ever. We were covering a war together and it was a toss up which would finish me first, the fighting natives or his interminable and boring stories about his exploits on the Normandy beaches. He was finally exposed as a complete charlatan by a telegram from the editor of the programme we were working for. As he read the cable he began to look worried and finally handed it to me. It said: "SEND INTERVIEW GENSITREP IMMEDIATEST."

"What's worrying you," I said.

"Who's this bloody General Sitrep we're supposed to interview? I've never heard of him," he replied.

This I decided was my heaven sent opportunity for revenge on all producers.

"Tell you what," I said, "we haven't got time to start chasing after this fellow. Send a cable back saying 'GENERAL SITREP NEVER GIVES INTERVIEWS.' "

He was on his way to the cable office with this message when he was stopped by a kindly cameraman. He took it like a sportsman. He never spoke to me again.

As I say, nowadays I take a more sympathetic view of producers. It would even be true to say that some of the breed are to be counted as my best friends. The fact is I feel sorry for them. I know that my seat in front of the camera is altogether more comfortable than their bed of nails behind it. Someone once defined television as "chewing gum for the eyes," and quite frankly I'd rather masticate it in public than make it private.

*"It's a great library—they **all** contain bottles."*

Mr Wonderful

By WILLIAM HARDCASTLE

I was given a bottle of *Brut* last Christmas but it hasn't done a damn thing for me. I was coming to the conclusion that my case was beyond the reach of even the most exotic after-shave. I was preparing to quit the starting-gate and go out to grass like some spavined selling-plater. Until one day I was mooning round a station bookstall and spotted a copy of that most worthy journal *Woman's Own*.

"Who are the world's most fascinating men?" the magazine's cover asked. I slapped down my bob and hurried to the station buffet for an elevenpenny cup of tea and an individual fruit pie. Over these, and a leisurely drag, I studied my purchase.

"When he bent to kiss my hand it was almost too much. Far from shattering my illusions, the real man was proving to be more overpowering than I'd ever imagined." Thus Miss Eleanor Harvey, normally one

of *Woman's Own's* most self-disciplined authoresses. And Rossano Brazzi.

I immediately saw a glimmer of hope. Maybe Rossano's pectorals haven't got the adipose layer that mine possess. His hair has to recede another couple of inches before it reaches the Hardcastle snow-line. But Rossano's been around this planet just about as long as I have. Our mileage must be roughly the same. Then I saw the "most fascinating" choice of another *Woman's Own* writer. Hers turned out to be Paul Getty, for Heaven's sake.

Hardcastle, I said to myself, you're back in the race and running. Maybe all I need is a *change* of after-shave.

But I paused and considered. What I (and presumably Rossano Brazzi and Paul Getty) have learned is that half-measures are never enough. A woman's magazine had given me a blinding revelation; it had snatched me back from the brink of despair. Brushing the last crumbs of the individual fruit pie from my lips I returned to the station bookstall to purchase the prescription that would complete my transformation—the *men's* magazines.

I was a stranger to this territory, but I had heard that *Playboy*, despite its title, was not a trade magazine for out of work male chorus dancers. I also knew that it sold billions of copies each month and enabled Mr. Hugh Hefner to have personalised rear-engined jets

like the rest of us have two-stroke lawn mowers. So at considerable cost (I went without baked beans on toast for tea that day) I bought it, and the magazine fell open at the picture of a girl with no clothes on in the middle of a rather damp-looking forest.

She appeared to be cunningly constructed of one of the more modern kinds of inflatable plastic. But anyway this sort of thing did not seem to be of practical assistance to me in my immediate problem. So I flipped the pages again and came upon a house advertisement which read, "What sort of man reads *Playboy*?" The answer apparently is "The guy with an eye for something special . . . in the decor of his bachelor pad or newly formed household."

Hefner, old chap, you may be making a bomb. Frankly I envy you your executive jets, even though I wonder what happens to your plastic stewardesses under pressurisation. But I warn you that you're missing the top end of the market—the people who have long departed their bachelor pads and whose households are as oldly formed as Stonehenge. I refer to Rossano Brazzi, Paul Getty and myself.

It was clear I'd got off on the wrong foot (or breast, I suppose you might say). To be fair *Playboy* is an alien product, and I had gathered that strenuous efforts have been made in recent years to build up—like computers, carbon fibres and British port-style wines—a strong domestic industry in this field. So back to the bookstall for further major expenditure (it meant doing without cheese and onion crisps with my brown ale later that same evening).

I have since completed my survey of the British male-magazine press. It seems to break down into three distinct categories. The first is for people who can't afford to go to Copenhagen and have to make do with what will pass muster by Scotland Yard's pornography squad, Mrs. Mary Whitehouse, the Home Office and W. H. Smith and Sons. In these publications the nudes are less plastic, the correspondence columns more neurotic, and the advertisements more explicit. For readers of this type of work, frustration and a dirty macintosh are essential.

The second category still features girls with no clothes on, but also stresses hairy-chested articles and fiction about motor car racing and grappling with grizzly bears. They are rather like *Reveille*, with knobs on, and I was touched by the free gift that came with a new man's magazine ("NEW—for today's man!") that came out during the period of my survey. It reminded me of the free German's spy's magnifying glass, and similar goodies, that used to be folded into the pages of the *Wizard*, *Rover* or *Hotspur* during my boyhood. In this case the gift was suitably masculine and adult—a money clip—but mine seems to have lost its virtue, and keeps falling off my money.

But I digress. The third category turned out to be

what I was really looking for. *Men in Vogue* (and it was clear from *Woman's Own* that Rossano, Paul and I *are* in vogue) is a magazine of severely practical advice.

"In the high income bracket, apart from all their gourmandising, very few men in the middle age group take any exercise. Self-driven or chauffeur driven, they move to and from their desks. Hey you, in your think tank, trapped in mounds of flesh, there's assistance if you want it!"

Thus, Miss Jessica Jessel, *Men in Vogue*'s expert on how to avoid the effect of advancing years ("Instant baby face can be yours for as little as two quid!")

"It's okay to drop your aitches," Miss Jessel avers, "but if anything visible droops or sags, you're better off dead."

Jessica, baby, you pull no punches. But are you right? You're certainly flying in the face of the judgment of *Woman's Own*. Paul Getty's face, to name but one, sags like a dejected bloodhound. But let us move on into the broader pastures of *Men in Vogue*.

Astonishingly enough this magazine has somehow managed to do exactly the same as its female equivalent and discover a group of male models in an advanced stage of emaciation. Certainly not the type to appeal to Miss Eleanor Harvey and the rest of the gang down at *Woman's Own*. They also get themselves up in some pretty odd duds. "Green linen thigh boot with grey snakeskin foot, held up by matching snakeskin waist belt." Not me, I thought.

As I wandered through these pages from yellow butterfly hat to bush suit in green velvet to trousers in cherry lambs' wool I began to wonder. Just to make sure I returned to *Woman's Own* and Miss Eleanor Harvey.

"The evening was warm, the moon was full. Suddenly I heard his voice calling a greeting. That voice—there is no mistaking it."

Exactly. Who needs *Men in Vogue* when a good pair of tonsils can do the job for you? Let me just add a point made by *Woman's Own* in its editorial.

"Why not drop us a line telling us who *your* dream man is, and the reason for your choice?"

Why not, indeed, though far be it from me to make any suggestions.

"They Don't Draw Like That Any More"

DAVID LANGDON cries into his beer

"Excuse me; what are those stripes on your arm for?"
"One for each time I was wounded, Mum."
"Dear me! How extraordinary that you should be wounded three times in the same place."

I grew up in a family ambiance of First World War lore and legend. As a schoolboy I made my own small contribution to the delayed resurgence of literature on the War in the late 1920s with an entry to an *Evening News* Competition in the form of an anecdote told me apparently in confidence by a trench-serving uncle.

To my delight it appeared in print with an illustration by Bert Thomas, and the family row which ensued (and I might add the rapid confiscation of the small cheque I received for The Best War Story Of The Week) did nothing to dispel the magic of that Bert Thomas drawing. I little knew then that I would be trying to emulate his First War efforts in a subsequent war, nor that I would come to know him in later life when his spry little figure matched his nimble line well into his eighties.

Fougasse was my next idol, both for his unique calligraphic style and as a mentor in my early association

"Hallo! — Yes?! — Yes?!! -

Yes?**! — Who is it?!!!—

WHO IS IT?!!!!! —

Oh . . . it's you . . .

My dear, how perfectly delightful to hear your voice!!!"

THE MAN WHO PAID OFF HIS OVERDRAFT

with *Punch*. The work of both these artists had a vitality beside which so much other drawing looked static and inert.

In the same genre was H. M. Bateman whose series "The Man Who" must be a major feature of any cartoon anthology. I don't think he took too kindly at his peak to us young tyros who were surfing along happily on the new simpliste wave which he and Fougasse had set in motion. I recall reading either a lecture of his or a letter to *The Times* rather petulantly casting doubt on our basic drawing ability and in particular criticising artists who when drawing a man in a soft hat showed the dent in the hat when the head was in *profile*. I for one took the hint and switched my little men from soft hats to bowlers.

Paul Crum and "Pont" follow next in my memory as

71

introducing a new element of fantasy and their untimely deaths were a sad blow to graphic humour, giving the drawings here an added poignancy. The way-out grotesqueries of a newer generation of cartoonists, in spite of their intentional shock effect, seem to lack the inherent comic genius of a Crum or a "Pont" and have, I feel, a built-in ephemera about them.

Caricature, that separate art form, sends me hastily back to Daumier and thence to David Low and Vicky. Even when their victims were immediately recognisable (Low once told me he spent months shadowing his subjects in clubs, pubs and restaurants like a detective before finally synthesising his caricatures) their names were often inscribed on their clothing to make doubly sure. Today's political cartoonists rightly disdain the use of labels but we are all too often left (with the notable exceptions of Trog, Illingworth, Garland, Horner) to guess the identity. Compare the bull's-eyes of J. H. Dowd (also a superb chronicler of small children) and his successor Bob Sherriffs in the minor field of cinema caricature in which *Punch* has specialised. Stylised they both were, certainly, pre-empting the reader's imagination, but true craftsmen.

"Strictly between ourselves I've been involved in some rather tiresome litigation."

THE BRITISH CHARACTER — Attitude towards Insomnia

"THE LAURELS" SEE IT THROUGH

My nostalgia too takes in the work of more formal artists. Struggling with the elusive science of perspective I was always riveted by the drawings of Arthur Watts. He plunged into complicated isometric projections of his own making with the glee of an urchin diving into his school swimming pool. The same joke can be put across to satisfy a modern audience without the elaborate detail and eye level, and anyway they don't make artists like that these days. Similarly I have always had a soft spot for W. A. Sillince, who made a bold bid for originality with his use of textured paper. His joke here is one of my special favourites—crisp, clear, copper-bottomed, the *Punch* equal (if we could cut the caption down to "What time's tea?") to any *New Yorker* classic.

With so much emphasis on the contemporary scene in modern cartooning and so little on timeless "pure" humour it is interesting to speculate how many of today's cartoons will merit the accolade of tomorrow's nostalgia.

"Well, what time shall we be back for tea?"

THE GOOD SHIP SURBITON

by THELWELL

"We thought we'd had it when a gale struck us on the M1."

"My back's gone again!"

74

"You single-handed chaps are all the same."

"*I'm* not going to be rescued by Bob and Vera Harrington."

"I still think Uffa's a damn silly name for a kid."

"Only *you* could get becalmed in sewage."

"Little Poppleford? It's in there somewhere."

ffolk

The Truth,
The Whole Truth
And Nothing But Trouble

The Nobel sentiments of Russia reviewed by GEORGE MIKES

About once in a decade the award of the Nobel Prize for Literature causes world-wide resentment: all other nations are deeply offended because one of their writers has failed to get it; the Russians are much more deeply offended because one of their writers has won it. If we go on like this, the Nobel Prize will prove itself to be more explosive than Nobel's other, comparatively innocent, invention, dynamite.

This anti-Nobel Prize resentment is a Russian tradition taken over from the Germans, like Marxism. In this case, however, it is not Karl Marx whom they follow but Adolf Hitler. When Karl von Ossietsky, whom the Nazis had imprisoned, was awarded the Nobel Peace Prize in 1935, Hitler was almost as furious as Mr. Brezhnev is today and forbade all Germans to accept Nobel Prizes ever again.

The relationship between Russia and the Nobel Prize people (the literary section of the Swedish Academy, in this case) started happily. In 1901, when it all began, Leo Tolstoy failed to get the Prize and the Russians were grateful. The whole world expected him to get it and the Russians dreaded this eventuality. The 1901 Committee were more tactful than the present one and the Prize went to a gentleman called Sully Prud-homme, President of the French Academy, completely forgotten by now but for the fact that he was the man preferred to Tolstoy. This happy relationship between

76

Russia and the Nobel Prize people suffered a hard knock when Boris Pasternak got the Prize in 1958 and was completely destroyed a few days ago when Alexander Solzhenitsyn was honoured. It is true that between these two insults, the Swedes tried to make amends by giving the Prize to Mikhail Sholokhov, remembering his great novel, concluded almost three decades before. But such feeble efforts just won't do.

I am no apologist for the Soviet Union but the Russians, for once, are of course completely in the right. Giving the Prize to Solzhenitsyn was what they like calling a "provocation." Literature in the Soviet Union is controlled by the Police: the Department for the Control of Literature and Pickpockets (DCLP). Pickpockets on the whole are nice, decent fellows, good Soviet patriots and give little trouble. It is the writers who cause all the annoyance, although the DCLP has clearly and repeatedly explained what is good literature and what isn't. It is all very simple: good literature must reflect life in the Soviet Union *as it is*. That's all. It is this rule against which Solzhenitsyn has repeatedly and gravely sinned. Not that he does not *know* better because the DCLP has often explained what life *really* is like in the Soviet Union: happy workers in explosive good health, grateful Marxists to the last man, walk along the streets, singing happy songs about the Communist Party while the wind blows their wavy hair. Solzhenitsyn who actually lives in the Soviet Union must know this perfectly well: he sees it every day.

There is only one other important rule: all literature must radiate optimism. And Solzhenitsyn, although repeatedly warned by the Writers' Union, failed to radiate. Everybody knows, for example, that there is no cancer in the Soviet Union. But Solzhenitsyn, ignoring the non-existence of cancer, wrote a whole novel about it. Even this deviation might have been forgiven if he had pictured cancer-wards *as they really are* or, officially, *as they really are not*. Nurses do not make love to patients: they attend to their duties cheerfully and then walk home through the streets of Moscow singing Party songs while the wind blows their wavy hair. Patients in Soviet wards are not downcast, they do not suffer, do not intrigue: they radiate optimism and get better and better every day with the help of Soviet medicine, doing its best under the guidance of the Communist (Bolshevik) Party of the Soviet Union. Before they die, usually of old age, they sing a Party song or two and the wind, blowing through the open windows, blows their wavy hair.

Similarly, everybody knows that there are no Labour Camps in the Soviet Union. Yet, Solzhenitsyn wrote two novels about such camps, just because he had managed somehow to spend eight years in them. An extremely selfish and utterly egoistic point of view: pushing his insignificant, personal experience in the foreground without mentioning it once—once in *two*

books!—how considerably the steel production in the Don basin was rising during those eight years and ignoring the fact that the people of Kazakhstan are consuming 2.8 per cent more goat meat than they did under the Czars. In his book on Labour Camps Solzhenitsyn completely fails to radiate optimism.

These camps are Corrective Training Camps where happy people do voluntary work for the benefit of the Communist (Bolshevik) Party of the Soviet Union. Helpful and wise warders sing (on the appropriate days) "Happy birthday to you" to the prisoners, followed by "He's a jolly good fellow," followed by one or two Party songs. The Siberian wind blows the wavy hair of the prisoners and the warders. Solzhenitsyn, obviously inspired and perhaps even paid by the imperialists, the CIA and NATO, painted a very different picture of these educational institutions. Little wonder that the CIA and NATO, using their well-known agents, the Swedish Academy, hurried to reward his services.

The British reader finds this a little hard to follow. Had Mr. George Brown's (as he then was) efforts failed to prevent Mr. Harold Wilson from establishing a one

"I know I'm working too hard, and probably killing myself, but I'm making so much money I can afford it."

"I wish to make a formal complaint about my new issue of office carpet."

"According to regulations, as a Grade II I'm entitled to . . . yes, sir, right away!"

man's dictatorship in this country, we would have here a similar situation by now. The only permitted literature would be the late Ivor Novello's musicals and Mrs. Wilson's poetry. (As it happens, for a few weeks nothing else but the latter was read in this country, in any case.) Mr. Graham Greene would be expelled from the Authors' Society for not radiating optimism, Miss Iris Murdoch's novels would be circulating in manuscript form only and I would be sent to an educational institution or camp as a punishment for this article, would sing songs praising Mr. Wilson's party and the wind would blow my wavy hair.

In short, the combined wickedness of Solzhenitsyn and the Swedish Academy has caused grave problems to all of us. Not that the position of the Swedish Academy is an easy one. They have been criticised during the last seven decades on various grounds. For political opportunism, for example. They gave the literary prize to Winston Churchill after the war and it was alleged that had Hitler won the war he would have received (and in spite of his prohibition, accepted) the Prize for *Mein Kampf*. The Academy was accused of courting first the anti-establishment writers in Russia (Pasternak award), then getting frightened and changed (Sholokhov award), then getting frightened and changed again (Solzhenitsyn award). They were also charged of favouring Scandinavian writers unduly and it was suggested that had these awards been given out by the Bulgarian Academy of Science, more Bulgarian and fewer Scandinavian authors would have been honoured. It has also been said that whenever an odd

"Kid, I hadda wait twenty years for my first bloodstained carpet!"

"This hotel was always popular with the old stars. Sir Douglas Fairbanks used to come here and stay in the chandelier."

member learns some freak, outlandish language, he goes on pestering his colleagues until an obscure poet in that freak, outlandish language gets the award. Otherwise why on earth did he bother to learn it? And so on, and so on.

The Academy is in an extremely difficult situation. The whole matter would be of little importance if it were only a question of literary glory. But a lot of money is involved and that makes it serious. The truth is that it is hard to find a man who gets and really *wants* the Prize. They always give it to people who are already rich and famous in any case and to whom the Nobel Prize matters little. They give it to Russians who are forced to reject it; they give it to M. Sartre who refuses it with scorn.

So we are in a pretty mess. Yet, there is a simple way

out. I hope all concerned will listen carefully and act accordingly.

(1) The Russians should let out Mr. Solzhenitsyn to collect his Nobel Prize in Stockholm. With £14,000 plus a million or two royalties already earned, there is a good chance that he will radiate a great deal more optimism.

(2) The Russians organise a huge march of the remaining members of the Writers' Union. They should march through the streets of Moscow, sing songs in praise of the Communist (Bolshevik) Party of the Soviet Union and let the wind blow their wavy hair.

(3) The Swedish Academy should give next year's Prize to me. I need both the publicity and the cash. I give them my solemn word, herewith, publicly, that I shall not reject their award with scorn.

In Praise of

SPIKE MILLIGAN continues our series of unfashionable crusades with several causes known only to himself.

What the hell are Punch playing at? Write something in *praise* of? In PRAISE Of??? Punch and its table carving gizzens think by acting like Drawcansir they can frighten me, a Gale force nine, into eulogising some grotty Anglo-Saxon gewgaw in print, by threatening me with money. If they think they can coax me from my grace and favour wheelchair with an offer of one hundred and fifty new pence they're sadly right. But *praise*. My God, it's taken this island race two thousand years of angry letters to the *Times* to eliminate anyone from being praiseworthy. Even as I write, scribes suffering emotional Xenophobia are about to shoot down the legend of Winston Churchill with a book entitled *Churchill, Warmonger, Alcoholic and Painter by Numbers* (Published Jonathan Cape £10 per volume but a mortgage can be arranged). At this moment throughout the world giant statues of past great Englishmen are being pulled down. Last year Clive, Queen Victoria and Lord Napier all went in to the melting pot in a Bombay Iron foundry the three of them coming out as a statue of Vishnu the Hindu Goddess of love. So who then for the accolade of praise? Forget the lofty halls of Power, look to the humble man and there we find my choice for praise. His name? Walter Cornelius. Not *the* Walter Cornelius, but *a* Walter Cornelius. Who was Mr. Cornelius? A quick reference to the *Guinness Book of Records* showed him to be the World's Champion Sausage Eater. Did he rest on his laurels? No. One day in November 1970, this man, living alone in a caravan near merry Peterborough, by trade a professional circus strong man and amateur sausage eater, without considering the cost, the risk, the political implications, decided the time had come for the first Englishman to fly under his own power. He fashioned a pair of large wings and patriotically painted them blue, yellow and orange. The blue was for the blue in The Red, White and ——, the yellow was for the yellow and the orange because he had a tin of it. On that cold November day he donned a pair of black leotards and a pair of wrestling boots, garbed for wrestling he avoided the obvious, instead, he mounted a ladder to the roof of a supermarket overlooking the partially polluted River Nene, on whose

bosom he had placed a man called Tom in a dinghy in case of mishaps.

Attaching strong rubber bands under his groins and armpits, he affixed them to the underside of the wings. Composing himself he leaped forward into the wind and actually did fly but downwards, fortunately the river broke his fall, when asked for a comment by the press he said "I've broken my bloody nose, next time I'll use stronger elastic." Did he cry? No. Did he blame the government? Did he threaten to jump to rule? Did he jump doing a full frontal nude? No. Nor did he solicit cheap publicity like Sir Francis who sailed a knitted yacht round the world on behalf of a large Commercial Group to prove that a seaman's underwear doesn't shrink in salt water and was knighted by the Queen who knew about seamen's underwear. Cornelius had access to myriad computations for capitalising on his efforts, think of the money he could have raised by writing B.P. SUPER on his left wing, leaving the right wing blank, marked open to offer, the mind boggles, it goes even further, the body the ears the teeth also boggle. He had but to put five pounds in sixpences into a phone box, dial the Kremlin and say "Give me fifty roubles and I will tell the press my flight was hi-jacked by Russian Jews who forced me to crash land in the river Nene." A man who turns his back on a fortune is my choice for Praise.

Second choice of praise.

Gandhi's Legs. Praise them. Why? Who will ever forget his visit to England in the turgid thirties, when a small frail wog appeared in London's social scene wearing a dothi, or dhoti, which ever be the correct spelling.

There was a young man called Gandhi
Who went in the bar for a Shandy
With his great loin cloth
He wiped off the froth
And the Barman said
  Blimey that's handy.

John Masefield should never have written that. It was the catalyst that sparked off the little wogs overthrow

80

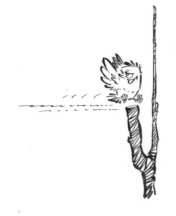

of British Emperialism. But, it was his little legs that did it. Compare them with the mighty legs of Lord Willingdon the then Viceroy of India (see photo taken with Felt-tip Pen). Who would have dreamed that those curry filled legs would oust for ever the mighty

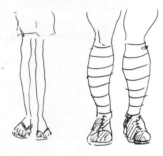

polo playing legs of the Raj. Those legs, insulted in every music hall in England, carried him on his long march to the coast to defy the salt tax. The Sahibs in the messes laughed. Those legs like dirty pipe cleaners would never last the journey in the punishing heat of an Indian Summer!

They would carbonise in the near heat and break off below the knee forcing Gandhi into premature impressions of Toulouse-Lautrec for a living. But! still smarting over the Masefield Limerick, Gandhi urged his legs on using ancient cries of encouragement like "Left Right Left Right, pick 'em up you black sod." As he neared the coast, the English feared a success. Snipers disguised as distant Hindu legs tried to pick them off, but even at fifty yards with telescopic sights the legs couldn't be seen. A second attempt to kill his legs by poisoning the roads failed due to heavy rains. He had offers, oh yes. MGM phoned, "Gandhi baby, I want your legs to play the lead opposite the legs of Mary Pickford," and Bata of Bombay offered him ten lacs of rupees to wear their footwear "The boot that kicked the British out of India." He could have retired for life but no, on to the coast where he took salt and with it the beginning of the end for the Empire. The toast is, Gandhi's legs! Next week, Mrs. Aida Scroake of Upper Dicker.

HARGREAVES

THE MONARCHY SHOW

By ANDREW DUNCAN

Next to the Roman Catholic church, the British royal family is the most enduring and successful show business troupe in the world. Adherents of both faiths—for the royal family is, as one of its members told me, replacing God in this largely un-Christian country—suspend reality and enjoy a mixture of hocus pocus, historical play acting, and contrived glamour that is the envy of every theatre and movie producer in the world.

The royal family is, of course, far more enjoyable than its competition. It causes no suffering and is, perhaps, the last of the harmless fantasies. If it demands a fair amount of hypocrisy to survive—well, that's show business. And showbiz has become the most effective part of Monarchy. Costumes, drama, music, animals, mysticism. You name it, the Monarchy show has it—or soon will have if public demand is great enough.

The central characters (Mum, Dad, serious son, lively daughter, two teeny boppers, assorted trendies and a sexy lady), are on permanent view. They parade throughout the world in a complexity of uniforms and guises to the greater glory of an institution and the country they represent—a limp wave here, a gracious nod there, a speech or two to keep the vox pop happy and satisfy the bureaucrats who write the script.

Stage hands are still drawn from the strata of British life that flits plummily between horses, hounds and bird slaughtering, and tends to confuse "opportunity" with "privilege." They believe implicitly in the show, if only because it has been such a long-running success. Changes in the formula are resisted. Even outdated acts, such as the Christmas broadcast, that have become parodies of themselves, can only be revised with the anguish reserved for tinkering with a Hamlet soliloquy.

And this is as it should be. The Monarchy show is not performed for London intellectuals or anarchists. Like *The Mousetrap* (and who, in London, meets anyone who has actually *seen* it?), it relies heavily on the coach trade. Let the cynics sneer. It will outlast them.

For one thing, it always adapts gently to its audience —hence last year's spectacular televised home movie designed to illustrate a "progressive" image.

For another, the real action remains largely unchanged. Like all the best shows, everyone knows what's going to happen, and everyone loves it. In Britain, the summer season is the most active. It begins with the Derby, meanders through the narcissism of Ascot and Lords and, with a few diversions, ends at Balmoral for an interval. The formula is easy, stylised, and successful.

The actors become bored because they have a life-long contract. Prince Philip, a vision of urbane discomfort in velvet, at the Garter ceremony. The Queen, dutifully practising to ride side saddle every morning for two weeks before Trooping the Colour. Princess Anne, off to yet another dreary lunch. Prince Charles,

taking an interest in one more esoteric aspect of national life. He, at least, is branching into a more overt form of showbiz—television interviewing. How they all hate it at times, but it's good for tourism.

The main London events, and some of the more flamboyant provincial exploits, are stage managed by the Duke of Norfolk, an improbable impresario whose apparent antiquity is contradicted by his success. The secret is simple. He is about the only man left in England who actually believes what he says, and one of the few organisers who doesn't see the Monarchy in terms of a game with the British people that has to be won by the aristocracy.

On tour, the cast is generally assembled by agents, called Lords Lieutenant, and organised by a leading local actor—a mayor, MP, or some such. During about six months of preparation, vanities are strewn by the wayside. The set, which can be anything from a single hospital to a whole village, is decorated with monumental thoroughness so that, for one afternoon at least, reality is ignored and a fairy tale can come true. The Monarchy show is no modern, slice-of-life play. It is escapist drama with historical pretensions and patriotic overtones—as advertised in the women's magazines and paid for out of rates. Sometimes an Arts Council grant should have been forthcoming.

Snobbery, naturally, thrives in such conditions, affecting the audience far more than the cast. At Buckingham Palace there is rigid enough distinction between various sectors, so that a senior telephone operator can be deputed to refuse calls from anyone but the stars and only be happy when connecting the Queen Mother with the Queen: "Your Majesty? Her Majesty, Your Majesty." But this is nothing compared with the attitude that overtakes bit part players. The

"Dad, when are you going to stop treating me like a child?"

83

more unimportant the extra, the more he confuses himself with the star, so that a local JP can strut for months with the remembrance of a regal handshake.

Sometimes the cast becomes so large and the props (in the form of official badges) so numerous, that confusion arises—often to the advantage of the posse of drama critics who follow the cavalcade in order to report any action. They have taken the place of Court Jesters in official hierarchy. On one occasion I had to leave a small Welsh village shortly before the Queen, in order to catch a train to London—an unforgivable act of *lèse-majesté*. As all the roads were closed to normal traffic, I hired a large black Humber, equipped with responsible looking chauffeur, stuck a Diners' Club credit card to the windscreen, and drove off, waving appropriately. Police along the route stood to attention and saluted. And I understood what it was like to be royal—until I reached the station and found the train delayed half an hour.

When the royal troupe goes abroad, as it does two or three times a year, there are more complicated arrangements. British diplomats, failed actors to a man, disconsolately sipping gin in some foreign land, set up complex rituals whose glory is somehow enhanced by the knowledge that they have remained unchanged for years. It always produces good theatre, and advertises the British Way Of Life.

If you tried to abolish it the howls from the shires would echo those from the slums. Who wants to be a party pooper, or shout "Boo" to an established success? Oh, no. In spite of the occasional boredom of both cast and audience, the Monarchy show must go on while the curtain calls last. And who can tell when they will end?

*"Not **another** broken bootlace, Miss Froblingham?"*

"When we first met he was tremendously rampant."

Bigger means Better

By WILLIAM DAVIS

The *Guardian's* man in Washington had the temerity the other day to call up our Embassy and ask what its nearly 700 staff could possibly find to do all day.

It is not the sort of question a leading British newspaper would have addressed to one of her Majesty's embassies twenty or thirty years ago, and I suppose it must be taken not only as a sign that the Guardian is not what it was, but that—alas—the Government's efforts to stamp out permissiveness have not, as yet, met with unqualified success. It is not for Punch to apologise to her Majesty's new Ambassador and his gallant 700 for this unwarranted intrusion into their private lives—though, of course, it grieves us deeply that a member of our honourable profession should have transgressed the bounds of common decency. What we can do, however, is to list a few facts of life for the benefit of other long-haired young journalists who may be similarly tempted to advertise their ignorance on the front page.

The Washington embassy told the *Guardian* that "the embassy's size is commensurate with its importance in representing British interests in the world's most powerful country." Well, "told the *Guardian*" is not, apparently, the right phrase. "Muttered with embarrassment" is what, according to the paper, the embassy spokesman actually did.

I don't see why. It has long been customary to measure a country's status by the size of its embassy. How else are the natives to tell whether a country is important or not?

Britain's empire was sustained largely by the huge embassies built by British rulers intimately acquainted with the ways of men. We were a small island, but as few people ever came to see us it hardly mattered. It was vastly more important that her

Majesty's Representatives abroad should look substantial. If Britain had a bigger embassy than, say, the United States it followed—for most natives—that we must be more important.

Much of the same principle has, of course, been applied by Kings and Emperors through the centuries. (And not only by them—why do you think Cardinal Wolsey built Hampton Court?) The initial outlay may be high, but in the long run it works out a good deal less expensive than, say, dispatching an army every time the natives get a little restless. A local chief or Minister (as I believe they are now called) was always greatly impressed when he stepped into a British embassy. Such splendour!

If the chandeliers and rich carpets didn't do the trick, there were usually a few large portraits of Wellington and Nelson in full military kit to remind them that the velvet glove hid an iron fist.

The *Guardian* would argue, I suppose, that this kind of approach no longer works in Washington, where the natives liberated themselves some time ago. Not so. The Americans still go around measuring everything. And I know, from personal observation, that they are much awed by the fact that the British Embassy is more substantial than the White House.

The simple answer to the *Guardian* man's inquiry, therefore, is that the 700 don't actually have to do *anything*. It is fairly obvious that, if you have a large embassy building, you have to have people to put in it. An empty embassy would still look magnificent, but it would almost certainly arouse suspicion.

Lord Cromer, then, needs both the embassy and the people to prove that we remain one of the world's most powerful nations. It is hard for Americans who visit the place to believe that we have lost the empire: the story tends to be dismissed as a rumour got up by journalists. Ambassadors from African and South American countries who pay Our Man a visit find the story still harder to credit. Their own embassies are, more often than not, scruffy little mansions well away from the centre of town. The furnishings are plain, the food is awful. When they complain to their Governments back home, they are informed that this is all their countries can afford. Is it surprising that, when they cross the threshold of the British embassy, they refuse to accept that anything has changed?

"*I've warned you before about your language.*"

86

"When I say pigmy, of course I don't mean intellectually."

Given these immense benefits, one could argue that, far from reducing the size of our embassies, we should make them even bigger. The extra rooms could, for most of the year, be let off to visiting British businessmen. If the rooms were divided by movable partitions, they could be made to disappear on important occasions—such as the traditional Queen's birthday party in June. At present, the Washington embassy cannot invite more than 2,500 guests to drink champagne and eat water-cress-and-tomato sandwiches in her Majesty's Honour. With a little planning, this number could be vastly increased.

It would also, of course, solve another problem which must be causing the Government much anxiety. At present, the Soviet Union outranks Britain with a somewhat larger score of accredited diplomats. (Most of our European friends only have half our number, and can therefore be ignored.) Largely because of this, the impression has gained ground in Washington that the Soviet Union could, perhaps, be more important than Britain. A bigger embassy would make it possible to add more people —and end this dangerous nonsense.

Keeping them occupied would not present any difficulty. The principal activities in the Washington diplomatic world are party-going, spying, and writing reports. All three have greatly expanded over the last few years, in line with the general increase in diplomatic representation.

Five or six years ago Britain's presence was required at not more than three or four parties a night. Today the number is at least twice as large. Failure to attend is invariably taken as an insult to the flag. (Foreign embassies even take offence if you ask for tomato juice.) This means that the British embassy has to have several party teams—and that, in fairness, it should be provided with enough additional party-goers to enable Lord Cromer to form suitably experienced back-up crews.

Spying is another area in which her Majesty's Ambassador could do with extra

staff. This is not so much because we ought to have more people in the Pentagon—the present number is quite adequate—but because it has become increasingly difficult to keep pace with US industrial progress. It is possible, these days, for an American manufacturer to invent, say, a new sprocket without Britain hearing about it until it is too late to steal the idea. Considering the importance attached to exports, this is clearly an unsatisfactory state of affairs.

Spying and party-going are preambles to the most important activity of all—the writing of reports. It is vital because, without reports, Whitehall would collapse. The whole elaborately constructed system—a system which, I hasten to add, has served us well for many years—depends on a steady flow of paper to the Ministry desks in London. It does not matter much what is in them; the main thing is to keep them coming, and in quantities commensurate with the growth of the civil service.

Lord Cromer, who took over a few days ago, has shown the way with a small, but generous personal gesture. He had taken his own cook with him. Lady Cromer has chipped in, too, by taking her own maid. This increases the total staff by two. Every little helps, but it seems monstrously unjust that his Lordship should bear the burden alone—especially as, according to one interviewer, he "shook his head, very sadly" when asked recently whether he was wealthy.

The existing domestic staff, it appears, includes a butler, three footmen, one doorman, one chauffeur, a housekeeper, a cook, a social secretary "and an undetermined number of laundrymaids and cleaners." In Washington social terms, this makes Lord Cromer virtually a pauper. One hardly dares think of what might happen if, say, Martha Mitchell happened to call on a day when the Ambassador's single butler is in bed with 'flu.

The blame for this lamentable—and highly undignified—situation has to be placed firmly where it belongs. Like everything else, it is wholly and exclusively the fault of Mr. Wilson and his colleagues—men who, I should add, were bailed out by Lord Cromer's banking friends on more than one occasion. It is not too late to make amends: the British public should insist on immediate action.

The *Guardian* would probably argue that, now that Britain has dropped her world role, we should be content with embassies similar to those of France or Germany. But then the *Guardian* has always been out of touch with reality.

"I'll be frank with you Watt, we're all a trifle disappointed at this new direction your steam engine experiments seem to have taken . . ."

ESCAPE TO PARADISE-ON-THAMES

The Population Explosion

will STANLEY REYNOLDS survive?

Please post me some effluent, spray some carbon monoxi[de] under my bedroom door or stop me in what ever way you will if you have heard t[his] before, but I seem to see through the smog of publicity that hoves over those tw[o] gods of the age, Overpopulation and Ecology, a slight contradiction. It came to [me] the other night as I lay awake listening to the night sounds of the new neighbou[rs'] herd of offspring and the drone of the boats on the river as their engines churn[ed] heroically against the flotsam and jetsam of pollution. Suddenly it occurred to [me] that the pollution of our environment will cancel out this population explosion thi[ng] and that the little swine screaming in the night above my head would undoubte[dly] choke on some new and horrid gases poisoning the atmosphere. Thus cheered [I] rolled over and slept until the morning feed.

Anyway, everyone it seems to me is worrying about nothing. The smog and the rest of the negative environmental impacts lounging about with intent in toda[y's] world is going to see us all right, so that even if the world's population doubles [by] the year 2006 the life expectancy will be so short that the population problem w[ill] be practically nil. 2006, incidentally, is no whimsical figure of mine, it is the da[te] they (sometimes known as them) have predicted that the population of the wor[ld] will reach 7 billion, and this is the conservative estimate; others have predict[ed] standing room only in some places, such as New York, Tokyo, and the 9.10 Charing Cross or something.

90

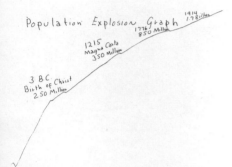

Population Explosion Graph
1914 / 1.7 Billion
1776 / 850 Million
1215 / Magna Carta / 350 Million
3 B.C. / Birth of Christ / 250 Million

I have some figures here that may not interest you but if you hold this page off at arms length or, better still, have your wife stand across the room and hold this page up to you, you will, I think, agree that this sort of graph thing gives the page a sort of weighty scientific air.

Now even the simplest of you can see it all in a nut shell. The population explosion is, in fact, so great that I ran out of paper shortly after 1914 and 1·7 billion people. I can assure you the line goes right on up and over the top of the paper. You will perhaps have also noticed that between the birth of Christ at 3 BC (which goes to show you just how much you can rely on figures) until 1215 and the signing of Magna Carta takes up about an inch and one half of my graph and during that inch and one half (or 38 millimetres) only 100 million new people were added, while in the quarter of an inch that divides 1215 from 1776 (the American Declaration of Independence in case you are curious), something like 500 million new people came along in just that quarter of an inch. I am not quite sure what a billion is—its definition depends on which side of the Atlantic you are on —but you can see on my graph that in the half inch (or 25 per cent of 38 mms) that separates 1776 from 1914 the population went to a breath taking 1·7 billion or 1·2 billion if you mistake my "7" for a "2" which often seems to happen.

Personally I am rather pleased about running out of paper because the increase in population gets pretty frightening around about 1944 and this is still, thank God, a family journal and there has been all too much reminding us these days of how babies get made thank you very much I'm sure. Anyway, the population figures are amazing enough to make you wonder if all that shaking will not throw the earth off its axis, and there are all sorts of natty statistics to go with it. There is, for example, that one about the population of Africa in 2006 that is pretty good but I just can't ever remember the punch line; perhaps if you hummed it to me I'd remember. It is something about the population of the world today being something something and the population of Africa in the year 2006 something something. It is, of course, all in the way you tell it.

One I do remember, however, and which I like very much and often sing in my bath tub is the one about the negative impact of the earth's life support systems. It seems some fellows have predicted that the US will increase its population by 75 million by the end of the century, and that this, is thought by some to be a very low figure and means that the population explosion will be over in America. But while everyone was feeling pretty good about this and slapping one another on the back and laughing someone else came up with this negative impact on the earth's life support systems thing and then everybody got very unhappy again and started walking around shuffling with their hands in their pockets.

The negative impact business is a new gauge for measuring how much of the earth a nation uses up. It is simply a variation on the old one about one of our boys being worth 20 Frogs, 40 Japs, and 50 Eye-ties. Americans, it seems, have 50 times the negative impact on the earth's life support systems than the average Indian—not Red Indian but Indian Indian. So, adding 75 million Americans to the world is just like adding 3·7 billion Indians to it and the graph I drew for that one was something to see.

What is good about this sort of thing is the way it can make you feel guilty. I mean to say, if you are not living in India and increasing the population 45·1 per

"Thank you, no, if I have another one now I won't get any praying done."

1,000 people by the year 2006, which is the sort of thing they evidently go in for over there when they are not whistling cobras out of baskets, but you are living in Darien, Connecticut, and you have 1·2 children and are careful not to throw litter about and only pollute the atmosphere on Sundays when you take the kids for a ride in the country you may not be feeling as guilty as you would like to feel but now this new negative impact ratio thing can let you feel guilty. In this country I would guess our negative impact while not being as high as America is still about 35 times that of the average Indian and so you can live in one room and hardly dare to breath out and still work up a good sense of guilt.

Guilt, I am sure, is the big thing behind all this pollution and overpopulation thing. I mean to say, nowadays they have taken away our guilt feelings about putting on dirty macs and sending away for Frou Frou sets (Paris inspired, a gay and frothy creation for fun time 45/- + 1/- p/p), and most people no longer believe in a God who is up there walking softly but carrying a big stick. You have got to have something to go in guilt and dread of and why not the hell of pollution and over-population?

Where people have slipped up is in not seeing that pollution will stop the over-population business. Just the same there are a lot of scare stories being put around by demographers, who are to population what ecologists are to pollution. One of them says that a very slight increase in population can upset everything—for example, 100 people may live by a stream and dump all manner of stuff into the water and still go happily along, but if 10 new people come along this could destroy the water (if those 10 new people are awfully piggy, I guess they mean). Or, the demographers say, two cities of one million each could be getting along just fine miles away from each other but along comes some smart alick and pops down a third city of one million people and although the population had only increased by 50 per cent the negative impact has increased 200 per cent. I don't really see how the demographers got that but that's what they say and they call it a synergism.

There is quite a bit that is sinister in the demographers copy. While never being actually bloodthirsty they are always complaining about the infant mortality rate dropping down and how people keep living into ripe old age. They can also get pretty harsh about the new drugs that stop epidemics. I imagine the demographers are just ordinary fellows who were butchers and plumbers and traffic wardens and public relations men before they went into demography the week before last, but taken all round I should say I'd rather get locked in a room full of ecologists any day.

Not that this population explosion business is not real, but how really does it hit me personally and how, short of drinking swamp water or driving blindfolded and blind drunk up a blind alley, can I beat it? One obviously will have to fight tooth and nail to preserve one's own pocket handkerchief of life-supporting environment.

There is an advertisement currently going around that shows a wide and empty stretch of tropical beach with the headline saying CAN YOU AFFORD TO BE ALONE? The idea behind this advert, I think, is that you pay some ridiculously low price and these people will fly you to this beach where you can be alone, providing not too many people answer the advert. That is getting away from it. There are also ways of keeping it away from you. There is the telly commercial about the fellow who everyone stays away from until his best friend tells him and this is perhaps cheaper than paying those people with the deserted beach to fly you there. It is, however, rather unwholesome. Perhaps a more natural approach would be to keep savage dogs or children; indeed a house full of badly brought up children, although adding ultimately to the population problem, is an easy way of curing the crush of outsiders.

Personally I should think one cranky old person about the house would do better, and would possibly do something to relieve the terrible problem of the aged poor. A pack of wild children eat and keep outgrowing their clothes while a grouchy old

"This is nothing, you should be here in the rush hour."

"There you are! Dressed to kill."

man will undoubtedly have no real teeth and if you hide his false ones on him he will quickly learn to subsist on mulch or gruel and will prove just as effective at keeping people away from you as a lot of children or, say, a brute of a dog who needs walking, particularly if you can get the old man to smell, which, I understand, is not too hard to do. Then, too, grouchy old men have years of experience behind them (that is why they are old) and will not need the constant instruction necessary to make a child truly disagreeable and repugnant enough to keep people away. The old person may indeed be grateful to you, especially if you let him know that unless he is nasty and boring to visitors you will hand him over to the demographers for shooting. Old grand-dads are cheap and if you look around you will probably find that one of them comes with your wife's family. Even the worst of children have a habit of falling asleep and looking cute while a good grouchy old crank, like the old grand-dads who inhabited my early years when ecology and overpopulation were unheard of, dribble and snore and sometimes even cackle horribly while snoozing in an armchair before company.

I have had several old grand-dads over the years and would match any one of them against any five kids any day in the week and twice on Sundays, which is the day grouchy grand-dads come into their own. A good one will be able to drive people away merely sitting in his chair saying things like "Bill Turner, no not that Bill Turner, the one from Oak Street, the one from Maple Street was his cousin, Ev Warner's brother-in-law" or cackling maliciously over the partial stroke he suffered in '28 and listing the names of all his mates who came to see him and thought he was a goner but who are all dead themselves now cackle wheeze. A child, on the other hand, has to run around making loud noises and saying "guess what?" and "you know what a boy said?" before every sentence for about an hour and a half before visitors will start coughing and looking for the place where they left their coats.

A performing child, of course, will beat a grand-dad. I used to regularly borrow little Pamela who used to live next door and who sang "California Here I Come," and "No, My Dear Franz" with amazingly hideous arm movements and gestures but the Harrisons moved away and a performing child is hard to come by nowadays, whereas old people are, as the demographers tell us, on the increase.

Still it may be a bit complicated getting in some old loon and if things continue the way they are going I rather suspect they will start putting the old folks down. I think the easiest thing to do would be to turn yourself into a sort of armchair demographer who will bore away anyone who comes within hearing distance of your amazingly boring statistics.

LIBERTY BODISS

"Yes, that's all very well, Brian, but is that such a steady job these days?"

Do We Need a Working Class?

Notes for a new revolution by MILES KINGTON

Once there was a time when things were quite simple. We just had three classes; upper, middle and lower. Then the sociologists came along and made everything complicated. Now we have four classes; upper, middle, lower and sociologists.

* * *

It is impossible to write an article about class without offending somebody. Usually one offends everybody *and* gets letters from one's parents saying that one's last article was in rather poor taste. So far this article has been dramatically successful, having offended only the sociologists.

So before I go any further I would like to say that the working class is absolutely fantastic and wonderful, and the same goes for both the other classes. I think we are lucky to have three such wonderful classes here in Britain. The title of this piece is an unfortunate printer's mistake; what I actually wrote was "Well Done Everybody!"

The function of the different classes is as follows. The lower classes do all the work. The middle classes do all the organising. The upper classes do at least behave beautifully. So who gets the time to throw all those bottles into my garden?

They are brown and smell of stale beer. If they are not collected soon, I shall throw them back. You have been warned.

* * *

Because I stated that the working classes do all the work I have already received several angry letters from disgusted ex-miners. Will you please have the courtesy to wait until the end of the article? Or I shall be forced to call the police and have you taken back to Merthyr Tydfil or wherever you come from. Bloody troublemakers the lot of you. And keep your bottles out of my garden.

As I was saying, the working class is the backbone of the nation. This means, of course, that there are a lot more of them than there are of us.

95

Good heavens, that slipped out when I wasn't thinking. I mean, there are a lot more of us than there are of them.

* * *

At this point I should stress that I am uniquely qualified to write this class study. My mother was an eminently middle-class person who always looked pained when I used the word "euphemism" and begged me to find a nice expression. She was married to a man so proletarian that he looked down on fish and chips as la-de-da; when he used four letter words it was with a bluntness that made it hard to believe there were as many as four letters in them. I have not referred to him as my father because there was some doubt as to whether I was sired by him or my mother's lover, Lord Grantoun, an exquisite aristocrat who would rather meet people he hated than soil his hands with a bargepole.

I am as a result, classless. For instance, I find it quite natural to spit when the habit takes me, and this I owe to Lord Grantoun. But when I do it, I spit with unerring accuracy which can only be attributed to my working-class father. The fact that, when I spit, I prefer to do it behind closed curtains in the dark I can thank my mother for. Sometimes I find the strain unbearable.

* * *

Dear mother and father,

I am sorry you are finding this article tasteless, but there are certain editorial reasons why I have to lie about my origins. Hope you are settling down all right in Cheltenham.

> (yours sincerely)
> (your son and heir)
> (luv)

If you have followed my reasoning correctly up to this point you will have realised that I have said nothing at all. People like you are a pain in the neck and should get the *New Statesman* every week to keep you out of trouble. I don't suppose you have been throwing bottles into my garden by any chance?

* * *

I had a very interesting chat last night with a sociologist I found throwing bottles into my garden. We talked about this and that for a while, then I idly asked him if he thought we needed a working class.

"What do you want it for?" he asked suspiciously.

"Not for anything special," I assured him. "Just in general. You know—would it save money if we didn't have one, could we get a magazine article out of it—that sort of thing."

"You're years out of date, aren't you?" he said. "The working class has almost disappeared already, but nobody's noticed. It always happens like that. Religion in the nineteenth century, for instance—the Victorian era was the most Christian you could imagine and twenty-five years later churches were empty. Same with aristocracy. One minute they're ruling the country, next moment they're opening the kitchen gardens to visitors."

"That's fascinating," I said. "May I ask your name?"

"Ambledale," he said. "Lord Ambledale, actually. I don't suppose you've got the price of a drink on you, have you?"

"We're making a sort of 'Easy Rider',
but for the older generation."

96

He's right, though. We don't say "what about the workers" any more. We say, what about the dockers, or nurses, or sociologists. The question we must ask is, have we still got a working class? And if not, who are all those people standing around outside my window? And why are they throwing bottles into my garden?

* * *

The working class must hang on to what it has got while there is still time. It must imitate the aristocracy, who have adapted one hundred per cent successfully to the twentieth century, and cash in on its assets, history and ceremony.

Question: if a worker threw his home open, would the aristocracy pay good money to come and gawp?

"We now come to the front room. It was here in 1913 that the third Mr. Tompkins fell heavily and broke the piece off the piano, which you can still see missing. The picture behind the door is 'Gypsy Maiden' by Woolworth's. Note the fine furniture which is all authentic London work of the mid-1920s. The ashtray, by contrast, is from Barcelona, where the fourth Mr. Tompkins purchased it on a tour of Europe. The lino-laying and curtain-hanging is all local workmanship."

Answer: No.

* * *

I have received an angry letter from a reader in the Pacific. When I say I received it, I actually found it in a bottle in my garden. It says: AM SHIPWRECKED ON ISO-LATED ATOLL—WILL HELP NEVER COME?—MAP REFER-ENCE FOLLOWS UNDER SEPARATE COVER—WEATHER LOVELY. As this hardly seemed relevant to a lively discussion of the class struggle, I was about to throw it away when I turned it over by accident and found more on the back:

"Incidentally, I'm surprised you didn't spot the flaws in Lord Ambledale's argument. It's quite true that the churches are empty but people are just as religious as they used to be—they're not religious about religion, that's all. As for the working class . . . ."

Here the paper ran out.

Went drinking with Lord Ambledale again last night. He has really led an amazing life. He confessed to me in confidence that he has not always been a Lord, in fact has never been a Lord, but that other sociologists are unduly impressed by titles.

I asked him if he would like to write an article for me on whether we need a working class.

"Couldn't do it, old boy," he said. "Sociology is a pure science; once you start doing it for money it becomes market research."

"Well, give me a few hints on the class system."

"Only too pleased. Always keep your hat on, never tip, and you won't go wrong."

Later in the evening I am afraid we got very drunk, went home and started throwing bottles in my garden.

"Of course I'll be careful, dear, and as soon as I've demolished the foe I'll streak home to you at super-speed."

WHAT WERE THE OLD DAYS

Marvellous! I worked a machine which pumped water out of a hole and pumped it back in again. I didn't ask questions. I just got on with the job.

I kept my place, too. We knew how to deal with discontented sewage workers in those days!

and you could drive for miles without seeing anything through the windscreen wipers but flowers and the odd cyclist.

Those were the days, of course, when one Englishman with a catapult was a match for any seven foreigners . . .

we had some pretty ingenious ideas as well.

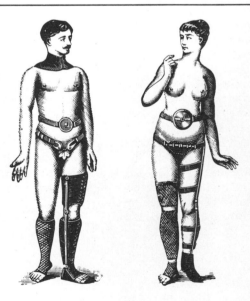

I'll admit that underwear tended to be a bit complicated . . .

REALLY LIKE, GRANDAD?

Everything was better then. Waiters were well-dressed and polite . . .

. . . waitresses always made you welcome . . .

. . . food was always fresh, not frozen or tinned . . .

. . . and the Royal Air Force kept the world at peace, leaving us free to . . .

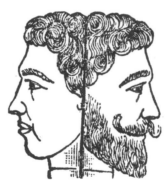

MOUSTACHES.

This engraving shows you clearly how, by using MR. DALMET'S POMADE, you may obtain magnificent Moustaches at any age, even at 15. Latest scientific discovery! Contains Asiatic herbs. Gives Moustaches to all! Age no object! No more boys! No more smooth faces at 30 years of age! All smart! Send at once 6d. in 1d. stamps to Mr. W. DALMET, 42, Gray's Inn Road, 42, London, W.C., for a box, plain cover. Send at once, as Mr. Dalmet could die with his secret. *Tried. Approved. Recommended to all. Send 6d.*

. . . make ourselves look good for a nice evening out. People today think they know all about sex, but believe me . . .

. but at least we always danced gether *and* provided our own ythm! Well, I've got a bit tired ith all this talking . . .

. . . so I'll be off upstairs . . .

. . . and into bed.

Honeymoon Hotel

by QUENTIN BLAKE

"Room 302 as usual, Madam."

"You know, it's funny to think you've probably never seen me before I've shaved in the morning."

"Frankly, we just see it as a way of getting away from the kids for a couple of weeks."

"I'm sorry, but rules are rules: no orders for breakfast taken after 9.30 p.m."

100

"See anything you fancy?"

The First Two Weeks are the Worst

Survive the honeymoon, reports ANN LESLIE, and your marriage can survive anything

ANN LESLIE, aged thirty and very glum about it too, has spent nine years in journalism and lives with her husband and cat in a bijou residence opposite the Peabody Buildings at the grottier end of Hampstead.

I'm told that along the rainswept pierheads of English summer-seasons, the damp souls of comics are still sprouting honeymoon stories, knowing that a joke about newly-weds has the effect of instantly galvanising old ladies in deckchairs—like hitting them on the knee with a hammer. "No, see, eh?, no, don't laugh, there was this honeymoon couple see . . . ooooh, *naughty*, I can see you darlin', put 'im *down* . . . anyway, this honeymoon couple . . ." Nudge, nudge, ho, ho. Maeve and Else cackle joyously through their toffomints remembering how Fred's mates at the bottle-works put frogs in Alice's wedding bed and gave her such a turn. In those days, honeymoons were epic events in one's life, something worthy of being laughed at . . .

Mind you, it was always working-class honeymoons which were supposed to be ipso facto screamingly funny: never upper-class ones. Working class honeymoons were spent in boarding houses with noisy bedsprings which rang out like tocsins across the prom. Upper class ones were apparently always Romantic, spent by limp-wristed young things called Charles and Amanda at Cap d'Antibes, surrounded by champagne buckets and portly Hungarians playing passionate fiddles under the trees. Curiously, sex didn't seem to come into the latter sort of honeymoon at all, whereas in the first type, it was the only thing that did.

But on the whole it looks as if the honeymoon joke is gradually losing its place in the joke-book pantheon, along with all those other sure-fire rib-ticklers, Scotsmen, sporrans, mother-in-law and public loos. Permissiveness has probably killed it off.

After all, the whole point of the honeymoon joke was that it was the First Time they'd Had It. Now, by all accounts, everyone's Had It almost as soon as they've cut their milk teeth.

I remember being told by one world-weary little thirteen year old in California, how much she deplored the declining moral standards of today's eight year olds. "Sex, sex, sex, that's all they ever think of. Why, when I was their age I was still playing with dolls" she said, as she popped Tuesday's pill out of its easy-dial packet and set off for another hair-bleaching session at the beauty salon.

Now *I* was brought up—ah, what innocent aeons ago—by nuns who told their spotty little charges that a man who Truly Loved you would Respect you until the wedding night, whereupon, apparently, appalling disrespect would take place, which was unfortunately

"Are you sure, Humphrey, that my little black low-cut clinging mini dress is a strong enough reason for marriage?"

101

the price you had to pay for the privilege of frying his fish-fingers and soaking his smalls for the rest of your days.

We heard a great deal about woman's Finer Feelings and man's Lower Instincts but never had a chance to put the theories to the test since the only males for miles around our convent were Ron, the scrofulous gardeners boy—and gloomy Father Flaherty, the parish priest, fresh from the bog, with a face like a fist, a hot line in hellfire, and a habit of tying his gloves to his wrists in case he lost them, so that during his passionate sermons on Fleshy Lust, they bobbed and weaved hysterically about his body like giant bees . . .

But nowadays of course it's all different and the whole sexual initiation part of a honeymoon has gone. Now the honeymoon is meant to be nothing less than a divine, star-spun interlude for you both before you get down to the real nitty-gritty of life among the Squezy mops in Spanland.

Of course, you're still supposed to spend most of it joyously tumbling about in bed together, only none of that beginner's stuff: it's got to be a really jazzy production number these days, real high-wire acrobatics. The whole thing imposes an intolerable strain on a couple who've only just managed to pull through the horrors of the wedding reception.

Most of my married friends swear they all came nearest to divorce during their honeymoons.

Like a girl-friend of mine who spent her wedding night tramping about Dawlish and district in the rain with a husband who said he swore he remembered the hotel they'd booked into was called Seaview, and for Christsake, stop moaning, there couldn't be more than twenty Seaviews in Dawlish, *could* there . . . Well, there could, and actually it was called Seacliffe, and by the time they got there Mrs. Potter said she was ever so

sorry but she'd disposed of the Bridal Suite to a commercial traveller, and some hours later the bride barked coldly at her spouse as she boarded the coach home to mother "I'm having THIS annulled for a start!"

Surviving the honeymoon is probably the first great hurdle in a marriage. I was once despatched to Canada on a ship which, my editor was erroneously informed, was a Honeymoon Special, groaning at the gunwhales with 1,500 emigrating newly-weds.

In fact there were four. The first couple had inadvertently been booked into separate cabins by the steamship company: she sharing with three Jehovah's Witnesses, and he with four members of a construction gang heading for Saskatchewan.

The other couple, who'd won their "dream" honeymoon in a cornflake contest, were together, but only just, as she spent most of the time being sick in the cabin while he glumly downed guinnesses and played shove ha-penny in the bar. Beneath us the wintry Atlantic heaved like a peptic whale. After a honeymoon like that, married life in Moose Jaw or Calgary could only be a blissful improvement . . .

Of course, the over-selling of honeymoons has even begun to worry social workers. One of them, the secretary of the Fulham and Hammersmith Citizens Advice Bureau, no less, recently quoted by the News of the World as blaming "honeymoon blues" for the break-up

"I'm so glad to meet you, Miss Rigby! My husband tells me he lusts after you constantly."

of so many young marriages. "The proceedings," she said, "aren't as romantic as they would like them to be."

Well of course not. Honeymoons are a time for the destruction of illusions, particularly those appertaining to the naturally dewy-fresh beauty of the bride. Before marriage you could maintain your beauty was a gift from God and didn't come expensively bottled by Max Factor.

Many's the young husband who must have suffered a cold frisson of fright on first glimpsing his wife minus eyebrows and eyelashes and all greased up like a Channel swimmer in Orange Skin Food. Of course, in America they've already thought of that, and the bride can buy sex-prufe lipstick, eyelashes and wigs, and in case you've got the sort of droopy boobs which hit your knees with a thud when you shed your bra, you can buy nightdresses with built-in foundation garments: "So soft, so subtle, He'll never Guess!"

To keep the illusion going, you can also book into that ultimate sexual depressant, the Honeymoon hotel, complete with heart-shaped bed, heart-shaped bath, heart-shaped swimming pool, heart-shaped skating rink, and heart-shaped jokes pinned over the dining room exits saying "We know where you're going!" Over the beds, there's a heart-shaped mirror so you can watch yourself in action, if, that is, you've got the heart for it any more . . .

The only honeymoon I've had so far doesn't encourage me to try another. Ever. We were married in Compton and squabbled furiously all the way down to our hotel in Midhurst.

On arrival, my husband, who puts his all into rows and consequently finds them very debilitating, sank exhausted with rage onto the fourposter and fell asleep, while I went downstairs and watched James Mason in "Five Fingers" on the hotel telly. Actually this was rather appropriate as I'd been in love with Mason for years and had always dreamt, while doodling on my Latin Primer, of spending my wedding night with James anyway. I once wrote him a poem in which I described his voice as "soft footfalls in the dark" which I thought amazingly good, but which inexplicably failed to bring him panting to my side. My husband had always felt the same way about Anne Bancroft, but well, there you are. James and Anne always seemed to be otherwise occupied, so we'd had to settle for each other instead.

The next day we flew to Switzerland to ski, where I promptly broke my leg, due to being hit by a tree which sprang out of the ski-slope, narrowly missing my husband but pole-axeing me. It probably knew I was on honeymoon. By then suffering from honeymooners' paranoia, I felt sure I heard it rattling its cones with sadistic glee as I passed out in a red haze at its feet.

I spent the rest of our honeymoon—all ten days of it

"*19, 20, 21, 22! Well, that settles it—it's not a salute!*"

—in a plaster-cast lying on a playdeck half way up an Alp wedged between motionless rows of old ladies wrapped in blankets mummifying in the sun, with plastic "beaks" sprouting from their sunglasses to save their noses from peeling. They resembled a lot of up-ended owls and none of them were great conversationalists—except for the lady who told me every day that she could forecast avalanches by the excruciating twinges she got in her lower intestine, and her friend, who apparently owned threequarters of Peru and had an understandable thing about Communists.

After three days of this, the sight of my husband, bronzed, merry, magnificent, shussing down the mountainside surrounded by gaily carolling girls made me long to shove him down a crevasse, hobble home and collect on the life insurance.

Things are improving now, but the honeymoon scars took some time to heal and I can't say I've ever quite forgiven him yet . . .

"I think it must be Christmas"

*" . . . but Dad, they didn't teach us how to fire Chinese
rockets at Sandhurst!"*

It's a long way
to Cannelloni

by ALAN COREN

**"The British soldier is becoming a gourmet. To wartime
soldiers brought up on bully beef stew, the Catering Corps
cookery book would seem unbelievable. It contains 1,076
recipes. But their resources will be tested to the full next
week, with the arrival in Aldershot of shooting teams from
all over the world for the Central Treaty Organisation
Small Arms Shooting Competition."**—*Sunday Telegraph*

In the dank dug-out, one candle flickered. The heavy air
reeked of fatigue and soaked serge and garlic and saltimbocca alla romana. Above,
along the odd duckboards, old ducks went up the line to death, to be stuffed, spitted,
sauced, and then forgotten. There had been some talk at Base of raising a memorial
to the Unknown Duck, when it was all over, but it would be a long time before that
day came. In the no-man's-land between the clattering mobile canteens and the
rat-tat-tat of the Kenwood .303 foodmixers, young pigs squealed horribly, and died.
The awful stink of burning flesh was everywhere.

At a makeshift chopping-table, Captain Stanhope sat over his cookery book, ball-
point poised. It wasn't easy to find the right words. Taramasalata, had the brigadier
said? Or was it tarragon? Or tagliatelle? They had all been out here too long.
Stanhope's eyes were ringed with dark shadows from too much stuffing; his fingers
were scored from dicing with carrots; his hair was falling out.

Sergeant Trotter, who had been there and back, and there again, and seen it all,

105

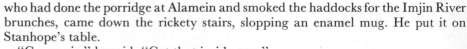

who had done the porridge at Alamein and smoked the haddocks for the Imjin River brunches, came down the rickety stairs, slopping an enamel mug. He put it on Stanhope's table.

"Go on, sir," he said. "Get that inside you."

Stanhope sipped the fragrant skate-liver-and-jasmine broth.

"He should have been back by now, Trotter."

"You can't never tell, sir. It's no good thinking the worst. Every cloud has a silver lining."

"Good old Trotter!" Stanhope, despite the heaviness breeding about his heart, laughed the brave young laugh that had carried him through so much, through a hundred collapsed soufflés and a thousand curdled bortschs. Stanhope had seen many flies in many soups. "Good old Trotter, you always know the right thing to say!"

"An apple a day keeps the doctor away, sir."

"God knows that's true, Trotter."

"Persil washes whiter, sir."

Stanhope sighed and nodded.

"Young Raleigh's a child, Trotter. He's only been with us two weeks. He doesn't have the experience. He doesn't have the nerves. They're sending them to us straight from domestic science school, Trotter."

"He'll make out, sir. He's got an old head on young shoulders, has Mr. Raleigh. A stitch in time saves nine, sir."

"I suppose you're right, Trotter. But he's never tackled more than a bread-and-butter pudding, or an apple crumble—and now he's out there facing the Turks with nothing more than a teenage sauce corporal and a few green private can-openers to help him. The Turks'll make mincemeat of them!"

"I had a recipe for human mincemeat once, sir," murmured Trotter, "it's not so bad. Don't you fret, sir. Many a mickle makes a muckle."

Erratic bootsteps thundered overhead, amid weak, sporadic cheering. Stanhope leapt up. As he did so, a fresh-faced youth burst through the doorway, his chef's hat awry and ketchup-stained, and flung himself into the dug-out.

"Raleigh!" cried Stanhope. "Thank God you're safe!"

The young lieutenant wiped his gravied hands on his apron. He looked hard into Stanhope's addled grey eyes.

"It's sheer bloody hell out there, sir!" he cried. "The Turks have broken through our fish pie and it's only a matter of minutes before they begin mopping up."

"God, they're filthy eaters!" muttered Stanhope.

"Give 'em a taste of cold veal!" cried Trotter. "He can't face cold veal, can't Johnny Turk!"

"What about our left flank, old chap?"

"Dreadful, sir," said Raleigh. "Complete bloody shambles. The French are

HARGREAVES

chucking everything they can think of at us—seventy-three orders of tête de veau vinaigrette, forty-eight entrecôtes de quatre saisons, including seventeen saignants, twenty-two bleu, nineteen without parsley, six with rosemary but no thyme, twelve with thyme but no basil, and nobody wants chips. My men are beginning to crack, sir. And I'm afraid the German assault on the knackwurst is beginning to tell—if the sauerkraut gives out, it's going to be impossible to hold them!"

"Dear God!" shouted Stanhope, "It's started earlier than any one anticipated!"

"You mean——?"

Stanhope hurled his ladle aside.

"Yes, Raleigh, it's the Big Push! And only this morning I had a dispatch rider up from Base saying that Intelligence reckoned we could hold 'em off with two-eggs-chips-sausage-and-beans for at least a week."

"What do they know at Base?" shrieked Raleigh, his slim frame trembling, "sitting around in their shiny kitchens, surrounded by clean Formica and remote-control cookers and waste-disposal units, making one another zabaglione and matelote de brochet au vin rosé? How long is it since any of them was out here, trying to prise the eye out of a sheep for a tableful of Iranian brass who'd have your leg for an hors d'oeuvres as soon as look at you?"

"Steady, old chap!" Stanhope's firm hand came down on Raleigh's lonely pip. Suddenly, an unhuman shriek rocked the dug-out, and a wild-eyed figure sprang through the Habitat beads, waving a Webley. He was dressed in a black tailcoat and a long white apron.

"It's Frobisher!" hissed Stanhope. "He's blown his top!"

"It's the waiting!" screamed Frobisher. "I can't stand it any more!"

"The waiting's always the worst, sir," said Trotter soothingly.

"Seven tables!" howled Frobisher, searching desperately for the trigger, "Two

"*Hold it, I said!*"

Spanish, two Greek, two Italian, and some madman sitting under the stairs who says he's from the IRA and if I don't bring him a plate of potatoes on the double he'll pull the pin and blow the entire canteen to bits."

"You've just been out here too long, old man," said Stanhope. "We all have."

"None of you has been what I've been through!" sobbed Frobisher. "You forget I'm only seconded to the 17th/21st Entrées. I came from the Queen's Own Yorkshire Light Sommeliers. We were a class mob, we could sniff a '47 Margaux from fifty paces, we could tell a Krug from a Bollinger with our gasmasks on, and there was always a half-bottle or two left over to slip up your pinny after they blew Last Post." His voice broke. "I'll teach those bastards at Command! What's a bloody bullet look like, for God's sake?" He poked frenziedly in the chamber with his corkscrew, sobbing and shaking. "I can't take any more!"

Stanhope drew Raleigh aside.

"I think it's an old omelette wound he sustained at the Royal Tournament," he muttered, "when we were trying to do a fines herbes against the clock. Never been the same since. I'd better get that thing away from him." He set his splendid jaw, reached quickly inside his battledress, and took out a small blue envelope. "Look, I wrote this to Molly when the first hors d'oeuvres started. It's my own recipe for gefilte fish au poivre. If anything happens to me, Raleigh, I'd like you to——"

Suddenly, with a frightful culinary oath, Frobisher hurled the gun aside.

"Useless bloody thing!" he shrieked. He wheeled, and sprang for the stairs. "It's quicker this way!"

"After him, Trotter!" cried Stanhope. "He's making straight for the Dutch front

"Hello, Dr. Spock. Say, I hate to bother you, but I've got this forty-year-old kid."

"If I had my time over again I'd do the same . . . except that I'd do it with Myrtle Higgins . . ."

tables, and you know what their appetite's like—they'll have an apple in his gob and a litre of sauce bearnaise running over his back before you can say Regulo Four!"

But it was not to be! An instant later, before even Trotter could unsheathe his trusty carvers, a weird and terrible multilingual din shook the dug-out and filled the gloom with unanswerable questions. Together, unhesitating, Stanhope and Raleigh leapt through the curtain, sprinted for the nearest dessert trench, and hurled themselves in. The air was full of flying onion rings and gnocchi, and prunes were everywhere. Gingerly, they pulled themselves up, and peered over the top. In time to see the khaki backsides of a dozen foreign regiments hurtling for the far horizon, the scattered victuals congealing in their wake.

"Dear Heavens!" cried Raleigh. "It's a bloody rout!"

"What happened?" shouted Stanhope. "What happened?"

A flying figure leapt the rim, and crashed beside them.

"Potter, sir, Sergeant I/C Soups and Cold Appetizers, it was Frobisher, sir, come on like a thing possessed, we couldn't stop him, sir. Before we knew what was happening, he was serving the French up hamburger waffles with jello, he was dishing out squid cous-cous to the Americans, he was hitting the Israelis with ham salads, he was serving haggis to the Dutch and raw roast beef to the Indians—I never seen nothing like it, sir, I never seen hard men break and run. I never seen commandos vomit."

A tear welled up and flashed in Stanhope's eye.

"Gentlemen in England now a-bed," he murmured, "shall think themselves accursed they were not here, Raleigh."

"Will he get a gong, sir?"

"Two, I shouldn't wonder," said Stanhope. "Lunch and dinner. He's saved the Catering Corps, Raleigh. Look at that!"

The broken foreigners had stopped, had turned, were shuffling humbly back. In the silence bellies rumbled, like far guns.

"Raleigh lad," said Stanhope, "order up two hundred cheese omelettes, and never mind about the rinds. I think our guests are just about ready for their lunch."

Country Life

Not everything that happens in Britain gets into the national press. This feature, to which readers contribute, presents some of the news which never made it.

Peering through the clouds of debris in his hall, he made out the shape of a lorry embedded in the front of his house. "I must admit it gave me quite a shock," said Mr. Dudley Woolgar. "I could see the chap in the cab and he looked a bit white. As my wife and I were having a cup of tea, we poured one out for him too."

(Portsmouth News)

Mrs. Maureen Trunks, of Costead Manor Road, Brentwood, who claimed that she had been raped by a Metropolitan policeman, admitted wasting police time today.

(Southend Standard)

Further inquiries are to be made into the whereabouts of the ox head a Wrexham man says he lent to the Borough Library in 1934.

(Wrexham Leader)

A bald cuckoo is being reared by two sparrows in the garden of Lower Common, Kerry, Montgomeryshire, the home of Mr. Jack Holloway. The cuckoo is bald because, as it has grown, it has filled the nest so adequately that the sparrows have had to stand on its head to feed it.

(Birmingham Evening Mail)

Mr. L. Brittain of 3 Cedar Drive, Thornton-in-Cleveland, asks us to say he has no connection with a manure smell in the village.

(Middlesbrough Evening Gazette)

A litter bin, buried in the hedge along Church Road, Kessingland, near Lowestoft, has not been emptied for 15 years. But, when the attention of Kessingland Parish Council was drawn to this situation it was discovered that the bin was only three-quarters full. The council unanimously agreed to wait until the bin was full before emptying it.

(East Anglian Daily Times)

The parish council at Moreton-in-Marsh has decided that there is nothing it can do about a complaint that ducks from the town's duck pond are walking around with dirty feet.

(Birmingham Mail)

Warwickshire Women's Institute will go on making jam but also involve themselves even more in questions of the day.

(Birmingham Mail)

The Bishop of Hertford, the Right Re[...] John Trillo, blessed thousands of s[...] worm eggs on the altar of Ayot S[...] Lawrence Parish Church on Saturd[...] afternoon.

(Welwyn Time[...])

A housewife of Spenser Avenue, Exete[...] sold a hired television set to a casu[...] caller who came to buy a budgeriga[...] Exeter magistrates were told yesterday[...]

(Exeter Express and Ech[...])

Mrs. Angela Cheney (76), who is soo[...] to have a book of poems publishe[...] gained her first serious poetic inspira[...] tion from a large puddle. It came to h[...] when she was aged 21 and living [...] Argyllshire, where a puddle in a roa[...] inspired her to write "The Sea Road."

(Hilsea New[...])

They met eight years ago when she wa[...] invited by Peter, a keen cricketer, [...] watch him play. But it was a damp d[...] and she decided not to go. They did n[...] meet again for some four to five yea[...] and became firm friends.

(Kentish Expres[...])

Nine hundred people danced around t[...] budgerigars in the De Montfort Ha[...] Leicester, last night.

(Leicester Mercur[...])

110

Lee Anthony Sargent was looking forward to his salmon sandwich on his way back from washing his hands, But he found his father had got there first so Lee shot him in the groin.

(*Leicester Mercury*)

Under the will of a local woman, Margate Library has received a bequest of ten cupboards full of sea-shells.

(*Christian Herald*)

Fletcher was sent for trial to Hampshire Quarter Sessions by Fareham magistrates yesterday on four charges. They were of stealing a set of ring spanners, property of the Post Office; stealing six sherry and six claret glasses; stealing two brassieres; and stealing a pair of pyjamas, all property of the Post Office.

(*Southern Evening Echo*)

"*It's all right, I've come to conserve you.*"

"*Perhaps he finds it easier to tread on them.*"

"Many people have asked me why I do this sort of thing. The simple answer is that I get more pleasure pushing someone on a wheelchair into the sea than I do just lying on a beach getting sunburned."

(*Evening Standard*)

"This man is no use to himself or to the community. He's a complete nuisance," Burgh prosecutor told Falkirk Burgh Court. Asked if he had anything to say for himself, Carson replied, "Yes, sir. What he said, that's just a matter of opinion, isn't it?"

(*Glasgow Evening Times*)

LIFESAVER life jacket for sale. Only worn once. Phone...

(*Sevenoaks Chronicle*)

The stone itself is not, as previously stated, a replica of a Celtic prince's burial stone of the 7th century, but is in fact a concrete slab to mark the site of a stone removed to the National Museum. Tegernacus, whom it commemorates, was of the 6th century and he was not a prince. The stone does not stand in the Gelligaer-Dowlais road, but is a short distance north of the chapel at Cefn Brithdir on another mountain.

(*Caerphilly and Rhymney Valley Advertiser*)

When two men stole six sheep from a farm at Mundford, they found that they could only get five of them in the back of their van. So the other one had to sit in the cab between the two men. But the men had to pass through Watton on their way home. They feared the sheep sitting in the cab would be conspicuous. So they 'disguised' it by putting a trilby on its head.

(*Eastern Evening News*)

Police who spent Saturday night and yesterday morning searching the rainswept Carrick Hills, south of Ayr, for a girl in distress found eventually that she may have been a rabbit.

(*Glasgow Herald*)

Mr. R. Horrill, a karate Black Belt, with a team of six helpers, demonstrated karate to Etwall W.R.V.S. Mother and Baby Club.

(*Derby Evening Telegraph*)

Mr. Lloyd said he went to the house at about 12.45 a.m. to return Mrs. Shefras's car. In view of the late hour, he stayed the night and slept with Mrs. Shefras.

(*Evening News*)

Costing clerk Mr. Raymond Wilks said last night that his figure of £50,000 as the value of the paintings stolen from his Chester flat last Friday was a snap valuation. Cheshire County Police had said earlier that five of the paintings stolen from his £5-a-week flat in Curzon Park North were the property of the landlord and estimated to be worth only £2 each.

(*Liverpool Echo*)

Mr. Jack Tooley, of Coleshill, a refuse collector and cess-pool emptier with Meriden Rural Council for 35 years, has been presented with a barometer by the Council.

(*Birmingham Mail*)

There was a good attendance at the meeting of the Bright and Happy Club in the War Memorial Hall on Tuesday. Members stood in silence in memory of Mrs. Luff who died recently.

(*Ashford and Kentish Express*)

The Beatles having now officially broken up, this, their last LP, has just been released

ELEANOR RIGBY

Ah, look at all the lonely Beatles.
Ah, look at all the lonely Beatles.

Mister McCartney issues a writ
From the farm where he spends every day
Hidden away.
John at his window, wearing the face
That his wife did the modelling for,
Chains up his door.

All the lonely Beatles, where have they all come from?
All the lonely Beatles, where do they all belong?

Look at George Harrison writing the words of a man
That no one can sing.
Doing his thing.
Look at him working, tuning a string in the night
When there's nobody there.
Does he still care?

All the lonely Beatles, where have they all come from?
All the lonely Beatles, where do they all belong?

Ringo Starr-Starkie went into films and was buried
Along with his name.
Nobody came.
Mister McCartney, wiping the dirt from his hands
As he walks from the court,
Has he sold short?

Ah, look at all the lonely Beatles.
Ah, look at all the lonely Beatles.

OH, I BELIEV

IXTY-FOUR

Vhen we get older, losing our hair,
week or so from now,
Vill you still be listening to our LPs?
r wondering "Why did we buy these?"
Vill Alan Freeman, will Jimmy Young,
lay us any more?
r will you just say "*Them?* They had their day
ack in '64"?

UCY IN THE SKY WITH DIAMONDS

icture yourself in a bank by the river,
Vith green paper trees and bright silver skies,
omebody calls you, you answer quite slowly,
teller with large copper eyes.
risp oblong flowers in blue and in brown,
owering over your head.
ook for the broker with cash in his bag,
nd he's gone.
ucy in the sky with diamonds,
ucy in the sky with diamonds.
Note: It has been suggested, especially considering the
le, that this lyric has something to do with the dreaded
s. d.)

ITH A LITTLE HELP FROM MY FRIENDS

Vhat would you do if I issued a writ,
ould you stand up and walk out on me?
uppose you had heard that I don't give a ****
ould you turn round and gang up on me?

ll turn rude, with a little help from my friends,
art a feud, with a little help from my friends,
nd get screwed, with a little help from my friends.

I'M A LOSER

We're the losers, we're the losers,
And we're not what we appeared to be.

For all the loot we picked up on the way,
What have we left to console us today?
We were a group in a million, my friend,
Who could have known we would lose in the end?

We're the losers, and we've lost something that's dear to us,
We're the losers, and it's only now made clear to us.

Although we laugh and we act like a clown,
Beneath this mask, we are wearing a frown.
Our shares are falling like rain from the sky,
Is it for them or ourselves that we cry?

We're the losers, and we've lost something that's dear to us,
We're the losers, and the shareholders all fear for us.

What did we do to deserve such a fate?
Served up ourselves to the world on a plate.
Became a piece of *Financial Times* chat,
And there was nowhere to go after that.

We're the losers, and we've lost something that's dear to us,
We're the losers, and you've heard the last you'll hear from us.

N YESTERDAY

"Look," they said, "suppose we put you on the cover?"

"It wouldn't," I said, "make any difference. You are looking, gentlemen, at a man who stands beyond vanity. Such bribery is risible."

"Full face," they wheedled, "plus written guarantee not to caricature worst features. Not," they added, quick as snakes, "that there are any."

It is pitiable to watch an editor with his back to the wall. Leaning for support on his managing-director. I sighed.

"I am tempted," I said. "Not for myself, you understand."

"Of course."

"For posterity."

"Exactly. For posterity."

"You'd need to have my name up there, too. Just so there was no confusion."

"Absolutely essential," they said. "So you'll do it, then?"

I sprinted frantically through my mind once more, poking in corners for honourable excuses. It is dark up there, and barren.

"Motor racing is extremely—how shall I put it?"

"Dangerous?"

"The very word!" I cried. "By God, you're not Editor for nothing!"

"You're not afraid, surely?"

"Ha, ha, ha!" I looked out of the window. "But I do have a wife and family. For my life, I count it not a whit, send me to the top of Everest, drop me over North Vietnam, cut my salary, what care I for such irrelevances, but think, gentlemen, of that innocent babe that grieving wid——"

"We'll insure you," said the managing-director, "for a hundred thousand."

I thought of my son, weeping as he drove off to Eton in his Lamborghini, of my wife gazing sadly from the afterdeck of her yacht at a jettyful of Riviera gigolos. Would they thank me for this sacrifice? I made a mental note not to ask them beforehand, and turned back to my sponsors, reft of argument.

"Very well," I said.

They went off to lunch, cackling sympathetically.

Fear, in fact, didn't come into it. Not physical fear, anyway. What really bothered me about the prospect of hurtling around Brands Hatch on a sliver of hopped-up tin was the confrontation it involved with my ego projection, and the irreparable harm it might do to those fine baroque fantasies that are the decor of my daydreaming interludes. Because motor racing triumph is the perennial Mittyism: we may not all dream, as Mitty did, of rounding the Horn in a Force Twelve gale, of dismantling Messerschmidts over Biggin, of unprecedented surgical coups—all these dream-feats require an enormous personality-shift into a totally unknown environment. We have not, after all, done a *bit* of abdominal surgery or a *bit* of aerial combat or a *bit* of trans-oceanic navigation, from which we may then fantasise by a simple extension of real experience. These other dreams are pure, unrealisable, ridiculous; and therefore safe. They don't intrude on our reality by making us wonder how we'd shape up to them, and our reality has no chance of intruding upon them: it is totally off the cards that I shall be called at some small hour to be told that the Prime Minister's liver has fallen out and would I come round sharpish and glue it back in.

114

By ALAN COREN

all actually believe that our not being Moss or Nuvolari is a mere accident of career. We all *could* have been. And in our fantasies, we all could be, still:

Silverstone, the British Grand Prix, morning sun winking off the assembled alloys, a vast and ogling crowd, the roar of engines ripping up from the grid, decolletage gleaming in the trackside rows, and suddenly, over the tannoy, breaks the news: OWING TO A SUDDEN BILIOUS ATTACK, JACKIE ICKX WILL NOT BE COMPETING! The echo dies in the groans of the crowd, the sun is dimmed— but stay! Who is this natty pinstriped figure working his way through the stands, vaulting the barrier like a Hemery, shouting into the stewards' ears, strapping goggles to his bowler, sliding into the vacant Ferrari, adjusting his mirror, stubbing his fag out on the manifold, blipping his throttle, snarling away, in front at the first bend, in front at the flag, a quick swig of Bollinger from the Mappin & Webb and into the sack with immeasurably succulent Lotte von Sachsenbrunner, one-time au pair and now just back from filming in Italy . . .

But we have all done a bit of driving, and we have all souped it up into daydream *in situ*: we have all of us slipped through the chicanes at Hyde Park Corner, out-diced an Alfa at Tolworth Roundabout, come close to smeary death at Newport Pagnell when that twit in the Rover, not realising that he was Brabham and we were Hill, wobbled suddenly as we took him on the inside. And we all believe that we are very, very good drivers indeed. It is as impossible to tell a man that he is a rotten driver as it is to tell him he's a rotten lover: these twin pillars hold up the gates to his insecurity. Kick out a brick from either, and the psychiatrists can start writing out their own cheques. And more than this: we

So there we all were, at Brands Hatch, novilleros of Motor Racing Stables Ltd., waiting for our call and wondering whether our fantasies would ever be the same again. There were a dozen of us, sitting on the wall beside the pits, in the autumn sun, kicking our heels, listening for our names to clang out of the loud-speakers; signifying that another MRS instructor was prepared to sit beside us as we shot round the circuit and earn his bread the hard way.

The other students enrolled in this mad course were obscenely young to be engaged in so dodgy an enter-prise (or so I thought; it subsequently turned out that I was obscenely old, having already reached an age at which most racing-drivers are prepared to retire to

"I told you we were wrong for Bristol!"

115

Geneva with a sackful of goodies from various advertising sugar-daddies and put their feet up on something buxom for the duration). Indeed, I was reminded of that other great cliché of the English male imagination, the Battle of Britain: teenage blond striplings, prepared to strap on helmets and embark on derring-do in flimsy single-seaters for death or glory, watched by an elderly thirty-year-old non-combatant group-captain with a pipe, a black labrador, and a tin leg, who had already done his Bit in another place and at another time, and to whom his squadron of brave skinny lads constantly refer as Uncle:

"Well, Uncle, bit of a show on this morning."
"Good weather for it, young Squibleigh."
"Wizard, Uncle! Taking a Lotus out, do a few laps, show 'em who's boss, knock a sec. or two off the record, nothing to worry about, back for lunch."
"Wish I could join you, God knows I do. But this old leg of mine (tap, tap) wouldn't stand the pace."
"Autobatic accident, wasn't it, Uncle?"
"That's right, old chap. Old open MG—what a young fool I was!—going through Burlington Arcade at eighty, out into Piccadilly, sharp left into an old Number Nine, all they found in the wreckage was half a spine and a glove compartment full of offal. Wonderful job of stitching old Sir Archie did, mind, but it put me out of combat driving for good . . ."

The only difference was that this time the poor old sod was actually going out with the teenagers. It did cross my mind, when the scramble call came out of the tannoy and the instructor approached across the tarmac, to tell him I had to go home to feed the labrador and oil the leg, but it was too late. I had already signed a form indemnifying Brands Hatch and stating my next-of-kin in the event of my being puréed against a tree, a helmet had been selected for me, the engine of the instruction car was ticking over softly, the youngsters were watching, incredulous of this crone, wondering, no doubt, if they would ever see him at some future Monza, coming up in their mirror at the helm of a Maserati propelled by three wheels and a crutch—it was too late for flight.

So I put on my helmet, which (like any other safety device) seemed twice as dangerous as the hazard it was designed to offset, and likely to shear my head off with its strap on the slightest provocation; smiled winningly at my passenger; and drove onto the track. Not since my driving test, fifteen years before, had I gone round with someone ticking things off a clipboard; and with nothing else to worry about except the unfamiliar car, the single-seaters that were arrowing all around us like whippets skirting a strolling ox, the assortment of flags waved by trackside well-wishers, blue, yellow, red, chequered, all meaning extremely important things that I had carefully forgotten, the five laps of Brands slipped by as smoothly and effortlessly as if I had been taking a pantechnicon up Snowdon in the wet.

The real hell was being unable to show my instructor what I could do, what fifteen years of urban driving experience had instilled into marrow and wrist and reflex; how to beat a pram to a zebra, say, how to slalom between the minis down Gloucester Place, how to cross Staines Bridge against the oncoming traffic, how to U-turn in the forecourt of the Hendon Odeon,

". . . And another safety feature—we've developed a very, very weak engine."

"I can remember the time when you could be pretty sure the butler had done it."

thereby beating the lights with the requisite three seconds in hand to catch the green at the North Circular junction, how to reverse down a motorway to pick up a missed turn-off, how to grovel for a dropped cigarette between the legs while at the same time preventing one child from pulling on the handbrake and the other from opening the back door, all those myriad skills beside which the tiny achievements of Fangio stand condemned for the irrelevances they are. Instead of the warm handshake, the glint in the envious eye that is the recognition of true greatness, all I got from the instructor was a pink sheet coldly entitled *Analysis Of Faults* and covered with libellous statements in a spidery, malicious hand. "Unable to double de-clutch," it sniggered, "Unable to heel-and-toe. Exceeded rev. limit on change down. Steering with one hand only."

"What's this?" I cried. "I was double de-clutching when you were still shoving Dinkies under your cot!"

"Well you didn't do it today," he said. "And you wouldn't get far on the Nurburgring with one arm hanging out of the car and the other one looking for your fags."

"It may interest you to know," I said, not wishing to pull rank, yet feeling the sprat should be put in his place, "that you are looking at a man who once towed a caravan to Dubrovnik and back."

"By horse," he said, "I hope."

He strolled away, no doubt for his weekly shave. I rejoined the students, who were all gibbering excitedly about their scores. No-one had less than eighty. Pleasantly, they enquired as to how I'd done. I demurred, with a smile of expertly gauged humility. The last thing I wished to instil in these midgets was over-confidence.

"Fifteen years behind the wheel," I murmured, "and you pick up a lot of little tricks."

"We'll knock 'em out of you," said the instructor, who had insinuated himself back into my life, unnoticed, "if it takes us ten years."

"I'd like to see this lot negotiate Trafalgar Square on New Year's Eve with nine drunks in the back and a stolen dog sitting in their lap!" I screamed calmly. "I'd like to see how far double de-clutching got 'em, coming back up the Bognor road on Whit Monday with the floor covered in crabs and four kids laying into one another with thermos flasks!"

We went off for briefing. This involved sitting in front of a blackboard on which a map of the circuit had been chalked and covered in cabbalistic runes. It was to be committed to memory before any of us was allowed into a single-seater. It involved such bizarre arcana as clipping-points and exit-lanes, and explained how one used the landmarks of the circuit—the 'o' in the Ferodo billboard, for example, or the line between a certain tree

and a certain straw-bale—to home in on the optimum course for covering the lap in the fewest possible seconds. It was not unlike painting by numbers: artistry via accuracy.

In short, no use whatever to an old hand who'd flown by the seat of more pants than they'd had hot dinners. We trooped back into the sunlight, down to the pits.

I turned out to be somewhat larger than the car. In order to build a Formula Ford single-seater, you take an aluminium tube, remove the cigar, and stick a wheel on each corner. Getting me into it involved a process exactly similar to getting a recalcitrant child into its high chair, i.e., you sort of thread the legs through first, bend them forcibly, then wedge the bum in with a short sharp shove, thereafter tucking in any bits left hanging out. Then you strap it in.

"Comfortable?" they enquired.

"Poor Herbert . . . he felt it his duty to stay with the car."

"Like the Man In The Iron Mask," I said. The pedals were the size of pinheads, the steering-wheel the diameter of a halfpenny, and a square millimetre covered the gate of all four gears. They started the engine, and, like a kamikaze pilot bound inexorably to his brief future, I took off.

Brands is a very short circuit, and each element—bend, hill, corner, straight—is inextricably linked, so that if you get one part wrong, however slightly, you're doomed to be ill-set for the next, which comes up far more quickly than you expect. I missed the Ferodo touchstone by a yard, over-corrected at the first bend and went into Druids as if I were actually coming back in the other direction from somewhere else. Yet, oddly, by the third lap, it was all actually working, I had reached a tenuous understanding with the car, and we were doing things together. It was a highly personal relationship; something to do, everything perhaps, with the snugness of the fit, so that one wasn't so much driving the car as activating the car-part of oneself, like an artificial limb.

And by the fifth lap, I was bored. Brands was so free of familiar hazard, all one had to do was keep the line and edge up the speed and that was the summit of achievement, knocking bits of seconds off each time around. No doubt it's different in a race, but on my run I missed the testing hazards of driving—where were the parked cars, with the doors flying open to disgorge housewives in one's path and the kids running out from between them after balls, where were the sudden crossing attendants, the ambers changing to red, the dogs and cats and loonies belting out of side streets, where were the swerving trucks and the U-turning cabs, and the learners bouncing from lane to lane, where were the distracting thighs twinkling along the pavement, the jams, where were all the things that make driving the complex and competitive joy it is?

I accepted the chequered flag, and I told them politely that I had enjoyed myself, and I gently turned down their offer to make me a racing driver ("Given time, of course," they said, and in their eyes I could see the dream of having this meal-ticket with them for the next twenty years), and I gave them back the helmet, and I said goodbye to all the budding Caracciolas who were eagerly signing themselves up for more, and I got back into my own car, and I drove out into Death Hill, and set a course for London.

Ahead lay the burgeoning rush hour, the boxes I was not to enter until my exit was clear, the police patrols, the Elephant & Castle roundabout, the million motorised psychopaths of London, the one-way systems, the fine, clogged short-cuts where one is ever on the *qui vive* to avoid dent and shatter, the mad motorways—above all, the thrilling *danger* of it all.

Ahead, friends, lay the real thing.

Standing on a Goalmine

A footballer isn't a footballer any more—he's also a writer, ad model, after-dinner speaker, fashion leader, product endorser and near-millionaire. We asked Lance Stevenage, one of the promoters who have made it all possible, to tell us about it.

Punch: Tell us about it.

Stevenage: Fine. Lovely. Shall I stand here?

Punch: We aren't using cameras. It's for a magazine.

Stevenage: Great. I love magazines. What do you want to know?

Punch: We'd like to interview you about promoting footballers.

Stevenage: I've got a better idea. Why not interview Clive Goodwin, the great goalkeeper? He'd look fantastic in your magazine, he says some killing things and he's yours for only £50 an hour. Is that a Grundig?

Punch: No, it's a pencil and notebook. Tell us about Goodwin.

Stevenage: You won't believe this, but when I first saw Clive he was a reserve goalie in the Third Division called Bert Stanley. I was doing my Tuesday round of East London dressing rooms and suddenly—there he was! This fantastic good-looker getting into a hand-made Italian suit. I could see his talent, flair and appeal a mile off. That was last December. Now he's in the First Division, earning £500 a week and driving a Porsche.

Punch: He let through five goals on Saturday.

Stevenage: What he does on the pitch is no concern of mine, though in complete confidence I'm getting him to cut down on the playing side of his career. Keep his Saturdays free for opening fetes and supermarkets.

Punch: Just a moment, though. I thought the whole idea was to turn football stars into celebrities, not to build up non-entities.

Stevenage: May I say how much I admire your masculine way with long words? Do you by any chance play football?

Punch: No.

Stevenage: Oh. Well, don't think we haven't tried. I personally have taken a First Division forward whose name, if I mentioned it, would bring you shrieking to the players' entrance, and tried to turn him into a sophisticated human being whom any compère would be proud to have giggling on his show.

Punch: And it didn't work?

Stevenage: We shall never know. Four months later he broke a leg and is now area manager for an electric bulb firm. Believe me, trying to get area managers of bulb firms on to TV shows is next to impossible, especially when they're self-conscious about their limp.

Punch: Who do you tip for the Cup?

Stevenage: Everton. Or Wrexham.

Punch: How does one promote a footballer?

Stevenage: It's like with a film. For years footballers were thought of as people who were clever with a ball, and films were seen as things you showed on a screen. Now it's different. A film today is also an LP, a book, TV previews, personal interviews, a luxury souvenir booklet, guest appearances. We can apply the same sort of process to footballers.

Punch: What does it entail in their case?

Stevenage: An LP, a book, TV previews, personal interviews, a luxury souvenir booklet, guest appearances.

Punch: At this point shall we hear something off Peter Bonetti's latest album?

Stevenage: I'd rather give a poetry reading from Clive Goodwin's column in the *Sun.*

Punch: That's a newspaper, isn't it?

Stevenage: Is it? Then why don't they print any news?

Punch: Because Nixon never poses in a bikini.

Stevenage: That's good! Are you *sure* you don't play for Arsenal?

Punch: What do you see as the virtues of modern footballers?

Stevenage: Sex appeal, good speaking voice, mother wit, legible signature and ability to appreciate promoter's wisdom, but not in that order. I saw Ian McKellen on TV the other night. If that guy had a crunching tackle he could be a great actor! Or do I mean footballer?

Punch: Bernard Shaw said that football was the art of packing the history of the world into ninety minutes.

Stevenage: He did? Tell Bernard Shaw to get his shorts on and come and see me, and he can open a supermarket any time he wants.

Punch: One final question. What is this bulky folder you are sliding into my hands?

Stevenage: It's an interview with me for you to print.

Punch: But I shall be writing out the interview from my notes.

Stevenage: By yourself? No help? No ghost-writers?

Punch: I shall be alone in the room when I do it.

Stevenage: Sir, you are a grievous loss to football.

In Praise of

STRIKES

ROBERT MORLEY champions the most unpopular cause of all

When is a strike not a strike? In my book, the Random House Dictionary of the English Language, eighty-five times out of eighty-six. The forty-first usage of "to strike," however, is given as "to leave off work, or stop working as a coercive measure, or as at the close of day." As a cowardly man, I flinch from the other eighty-five definitions. I am in favour of leaving off work at the close of day, earlier if possible. I have never been able to work myself up about the folly and wickedness of industrial action, any more than I have been able to excite myself about the economy, the balance of payments or the growth rate of industry or the human race.

As a child I used to visit a donkey at Carisbrooke Castle who spent his working hours inside a giant wheel, trying to get somewhere. As the wheel revolved, water was drawn from a well. Other tourists and the brute's guardian purported to believe that the donkey was making a conscious effort to improve the water supply, but I was convinced that he was merely trying to stay put. I found nothing to admire about the poor beast, but I had a sneaking admiration for the inventor of the wheel. However, there was always a doubt in my mind that Neddy was really enjoying himself. Supposing he stopped, supposing he struck! Reminded his captors that he had been born to enjoy green grass and gracious living! Would they confiscate his food, his bed, his water! I don't imagine they would want to risk prosecution by the RSPCA. They would be more likely to shoot the poor brute and buy a pump, or of course another donkey. There has never been a shortage of donkeys.

The classical dilemma of the worker is that, while it is boring to go on, it is equally boring to stop altogether. The solution, therefore, is to stop for a breather, hence the popularity of strikes. If a man works at a job which totally bores him, life itself becomes meaningless and

his world, like the donkey's, a treadmill. A blue sky, a cold sea, a slippery slope, a desert, an oasis, a hill, a valley, an island, a continent, each is unobserved by him. In a world in which men and donkeys come in all shapes and sizes, in which no mould is ever repeated, except in the case of identical twins, in which no two views are ever alike, the colour of each blade of grass differs one from the other, and every pebble on the beach is separate and distinct; such a man, his eyes shut tight, his lips pursed, his ears deafened, is engaged in the task of car spraying, taking pains that every car should look as much like the last as possible, defying Nature, defeating himself. Such a man should lie down and be carried off on his own assembly line.

Man, unlike the animals, has never learnt to understand or appreciate his environment. The best times are had by butterflies and bears, possums are happy, but not man. Cats are content, but not man. I never think dogs are happy, but that is perhaps because I am never happy with them. Pheasants look happy, but not the Duke of Edinburgh when he is trying to shoot them. Mention of pheasants reminds me of the saddest of all sitting ducks—the Secretary Bird. At least the postal strike has brought her momentary relief. There can be few more depressing human predicaments than to sit for hours on end, listening to business men calling to one another, or to have to perpetuate the banalities of commercial correspondence on crisp notepaper with a carbon copy beneath. In our society, battery hens are more kindly treated than audio-typists.

I too have enjoyed the postal strike, indeed, as I write this, am still enjoying it hugely. Letters have brought me little happiness in the past. The ones I have written were largely a waste of my time and effort, the ones I received scarcely worth perusing, let alone preserving. I don't say I haven't experienced an occasional warm flush over the panegyrics of a fan from Bourne-

mouth, but equally I have experienced despair over a communication from my bookmaker. I have written a good deal of nonsense, and read even more. I have endured the flattery of investment advisors, the ravings of religious fanatics, the ceaseless admonitions of accountants. I have wasted months of my life turning the pages of the catalogues of art dealers, silversmiths, Dutch bulb growers, department stores and makers of burglar alarms. There are times when it has seemed to me that no church fete could take place up or down the country without an appeal to me to send an article of personal apparel, or a thumb print. Why should a man who is willing to pay half-a-crown to help restore an eighteenth-century pulpit in Blackburn be lumbered with my signature scrawled on a postcard? It is marvellous to wake up, even on these winter mornings, and realise one cannot possibly receive a personal appeal from Lord Louis Mountbatten or Peter Scott, or find that one has been selected by the *Reader's Digest* as a recipient of their largesse.

When at last, unable to resist the entreaties of my fellow citizens any longer, I am dragged in token reluc-tance to the seat of power, I shall make it a criminal offence for anyone to possess a typewriter, to dictate a letter or write to someone they do not know personally. I shall also make it mandatory for all workers to strike for at least a month each year. The public will have the excitement of a milkless month, a meatless month, a lawless month, a paperless month, a televisionless month, and so on. It will be able to break the monotony of the Sunday joint and the daily pinta and recapture for itself temporarily at any rate the pleasures that it has forgotten—candlelight, exercise, silence, conversation. It will learn independence and commonsense once more.

There is only one definition of commonsense in the Random House Dictionary—"sound practical judgment that is independent of specialised knowledge, training, or the like; normal, native intelligence." How, you may ask, now that my secretary has typed this offering, am I to ensure that it reaches the offices of *Punch*? Normal native intelligence insists that I should entrust it to my chauffeur.

"One last question—how would you handle the student protest sit-in that would be inevitable on your appointment?"

Bureaucrat At Home *by* GRAHAM

"Had a marvellous day . . . turned down four appeals under good old sub-section twenty-nine."

"The Minister did you say?"

"Mum gave us planning permission."

"Take a post-card."

ingside . . . Geoffrey Morningside . . .
y Morningside, O.B.E., actually."

"While not unsympathetic to your request,
I regret that the vehicle under discussion
will be in use to convey your mother and
me to the Simpson's party."

If My Memories Serve Me Right

By JOHN TAYLOR

Just over a quarter of a century ago, at the age of 23, I became a national institution by being rotten to Herbert Morrison.

Like most great feats of reputational journalism, it was quite unconsidered at the time. A photographic agency had mistakenly dispatched me a couple of pictures of Herbert departing on a diplomatic journey somewhere and returning a few days later. In both pictures he was clearly wearing the same suit and in the second he seemed utterly devoid of all the elegances of valeting.

Press time was galloping towards me with an empty page of *The Tailor and Cutter* still lying there helpless—and I decided to rock the throne. Beneath the *Hamlet* heading "Look here upon this picture, and on this . . ." I chided Mr. Morrison for his lack of responsibility as a public citizen, criticised the style of the suit, suggested improvements such as ". . . more starch in the collar and a little less in the diet . . ." and carried on generally.

On the day after publication I was startled to taste the doubtful pleasure of professional harlotry—power without responsibility. An eagle-eyed PA man pushed the story on to the wire and it was picked up around the world.

Seeing my name in every national and weekly as the Durrant's clippings rolled in frightened the life out of me and I hastily regretted a touch of whimsy which had seemed like a good idea at the time. Furthermore, Herbert Morrison's tailor, a Mr. Grey of the Co-operative Wholesale Society, took the train down from Newcastle expressly to offer to kick my arse around the block. I partly mollified him with an apéritif at the York Minster (a pub he came to use regularly on visits to London during the many years that followed), but his initial fury, coupled with an uneasy feeling that Herbert might have my head cut off, decided for me that Fame was not really my scene.

But no journalist ever *really* learned a lesson. The delight of knocking the Establishment, the egotistic pleasures of iconoclasm, once experienced, hook a man. Within a year I had sartorially crucified the Duke of Windsor, Leonard Hutton, the Poet Laureate, and a symposium of national newspaper critics—despite the professional injunction that dog didn't eat dog. Bernard

"*I think it only fair to warn you that I was once a teddy-boy.*"

124

"Of course your umbrella didn't open. It's not supposed to open. You're a clown, aren't you?"

Shaw even replied on one of his postcards, defending himself with the insistence that he had worn "coloured collars before anyone else ever dared . . ."

To be truthful, I had suspected the power of personal projection dormant in clothing when I had first applied for the job of Editor of *The T and C*. On indefinite leave pending demobilisation from the Fleet Air Arm, I had answered an ad. in the old *World's Press News* (now *Campaign*) and had presented myself in a neat lounge suit as seeming to be suitable to the application. I learned in later years that I was turned down because six years of service life had filled me out to a point where it threatened to split.

About four months later, now demobilised, I saw an almost identical advertisement in the same paper and re-presented myself, this time in uniform.

Marcus Smith, the then Chairman, was impressed enough by my gold braid, my Fleet Air Arm pilot's wings, a row of medal ribbons of whose inconsequential

character he wotted not, and my apocryphal claim to be 27 years old, to offer me the job. He was not impressed enough, however, to offer me more than £8 10s. a week.

If £8 10s. a week doesn't seem very much today, it is possibly because it didn't seem very much in those days either—so whilst I was at the time probably the youngest editor in the country, I was certainly the cheapest.

In the early years of my responsibility, especially when I was under the age of 30, I took it all very very seriously. Convinced that my duty was towards the stark projection of subfusc rectitude, I would garb myself in grotesque formality at the drop of a Bowler. I recall with unease to this day having made for me a four-button single breasted, black jacket which I wore with a pair of black and white, large-checked, trousers; a high stiff collar; a white knitted tie with a pearl stick-pin; a double breasted waistcoat to match the trousers; and a scarlet carnation. I must have looked at best like

125

something out of the Chorus, at worst like a prize berk.

In the West End, of course, it was easy to look a little absurd without inducing too much hostility. But travelling up to town daily from Tunbridge Wells was more of an ordeal. Normally dressed men from insurance firms and banks would edge away and lower their voices when I walked on to the platform, convinced I was a professional homosexual who plied his trade daily in the metropolis.

I put up with it all as the price of fame, but youth is all sensitivity. Determined never to let my public image down, I recall once borrowing a pearl grey morning suit from the Brothers Moss to enliven the wedding of a friend's daughter—and rectifying the slightly too long trousers by adjusting the braces to their maximum point of tightness.

I had been standing at the Champagne bar for no more than 20 minutes when a sharp pain stabbed into my left forearm and steadily began to explore my bicep, elbow, shoulder, and fingers. The pain was followed, to my intense dismay, with a creeping pins-and-needles which finally rendered the whole arm numb.

Hardly had the perspiration broken coldly on my forehead when a similar phenomenon began to attack the other arm stabbing down till I was left holding my glass in nerveless fingers.

"This is it!" I told myself in a simulation of fatalistic courage. I knew the pain and deadness had but to spread across my chest till it met in the middle and BINGO! My horror was mitigated only at a curious pride at dying with a glass in my hand.

The misery of the occasion was explained only when, on returning home, I slipped off my braces and the warm blood flooded back down my empty arms with all the agony of retreating frost bite. It is perhaps the only recorded instance of a man losing the power of his arms through a too long pair of trousers.

Some of the stresses of responsibility were mental rather than physical. A too casual reaction to the Roman climate brought me to a point where I was once refused admission to the restaurant of the Majestic Hotel on the Via Veneto because I was not wearing a tie.

I was accompanied by two companions at the time— one Howard Thomas, the television mogul, and the other Leslie Beckett then the editor of my dreaded rival *Men's Wear*; who were both admitted.

Initial chagrin gave way to deep anxiety as I envisaged the international reaction if the story broke:

FASHION AUTHORITY GETS BUM'S RUSH,

or, ARBITER ELEGANTIARUM BOUNCED FROM TOP NITERY.

Ignorance No Excuse, says Judge.

All these danced before sleepless eyes for many a night whilst I wondered if Leslie might print the story. True to the tradition of dog not eating dog he didn't, and Howard's silence was bought with a Campari Soda

—but the torture I suffered was indicative of my deeply brain-washed attitudes in those days.

Only the years brought to me a feeling that as the Authority I could do what I wanted. Or was it that the spread of casual fashion at last brought sartorial acceptances more in keeping with the slob inside me which had tried to get out for so many years?

Realisation that my iconoclasm was at last turning into perversity came only three or four years ago when I had driven up to the TV centre to appear on a New Year's Eve programme forecasting the fashions for the coming year. No longer over conscious of my image I had conceded to a freezing day by wearing a great ragged sheepskin coat which I have loved for many years and which waggish friends have christened The Gnu Look. Looking as though some wild beast had me already half digested I parked the car and made for reception.

I lit a cigarette idly whilst waiting for the inevitable Programme Secretary to appear and lead me through the labyrinths; and was interested to see the lift doors suddenly open and disgorge Milton Shulman—Critic, Producer, Author, Atmospheric Policeman and Purple People Eater of the TV Set.

Sweeping the front hall, his eyes came to rest on me at last, and raising his hand in a gesture of acknowledgement he began to walk towards me.

I was flattered. I had long admired but never met the man—and as he stamped across the lobby towards me I inwardly applauded this charming *camaraderie* of one famous and authoritative journalist towards another.

Arriving at last, he acknowledged my great loony grin of welcome with a curt nod and enquired (not unkindly, you understand) "Are you my cab?"

In that instant I suddenly realised that it was time to move on and edit another magazine.

Some of us never pay attention to or think about royalty or anything else, for that matter.

If certain Britons have their way, the royal family might find themselves unemployed. They could emigrate to the United States—starting a Brougham Drain. Their chances of finding work—and general acceptance of them—would depend on certain attitudes already existing among us, says America's Arnold Roth.

Her Majesty should be forewarned that certain individuals are still angry at her great-great-great-great grandfather and his crowd.

(continued overleaf)

A modicum of adjustment might be necessary for all concerned.

There are people here who have little respect for anything.

Longed-for thrills could be provided for those of our humble citizens who want for nothing.

We do desperately need a full-time functionary who would free the President to concentrate all his energies on ruining the nation.

Many fans would bring to the royal presence a kind of dedication which only converts possess.

Well, Hard Luck...

By ALAN HACKNEY

"God knows I've tried—but I just simply do not feel European."

Reuters report that a M. Armand Portnoy, a French garage worker, has complained to a Paris court about the novel "Portnoy's Complaint." He is asking for the book to be banned in France as it has "made him the target of offensive jokes."

Pope Paul VI,
The Vatican, Rome, Italy.

Your Holiness,

I make this appeal after many years of personal anguish, hoping you will understand my position and help to rectify same.

People identifying me with a character in the widely published book known as the "New Testament" have brought me into hatred, ridicule and contempt for a number of years. Mostly ridicule, with such remarks as: "Still around? Thought you were supposed to have hanged yourself, years ago," or "How much for the job, then? Thirty pieces of silver, ha, ha, ha?" As I am in the business of French polishing which is anyway what is known as a dying trade, with nothing near the amount of work there was, the extra drop in business due to prejudice makes it more uphill than it need be, and although I conduct the business under a trade name, namely Ace Polishers, when I am asked to sign a receipt I am up the spout.

To any suggestion I should put in to have my name changed, apart from not feeling able to afford it with the trade the way it is, I would say, No, why should I, it is not up to me.

No, your Holy Father, this is something you could do to help me, without much trouble. I have seen in the press you managed to ban the worship of various saints like St. Christopher and St. Philomena because research has shown it was very doubtful if they really existed. All I ask is a bit more research, to come up with a similar ban on someone nobody is going to grieve over, especially

yours truly, with respect,
JUDAS ISCARIOT,
283 High Street, London S.E.29.

"It's astonishing how personal possessions accumulate!"

To: Action Line, *Daily Express.*

Dear Action Line,

I am trying you after everything else I have tried has failed, hoping you can help me, as you are in the newspaper business.

Usually I lead a quiet life, but every couple of years or so various newspapers keep dragging in feature articles, each more sensational than the last, going into details about a person who is no relation, under titles like "The Mad Monk of Russia," "The Bearded Beast of Moscow" and so on. Surely there are other pleasanter subjects readers would welcome, such as articles on gardening, holidays in the sun, etc., which papers could print when they are short of news? There is enough nastiness as it is.

As it is, I live in dread of opening my paper and finding yet another reminder to friends and neighbours that I have the misfortune to bear a name best forgotten.

I have never been to Russia and am a loyal anti-Communist. Also I am against the Common Market which will not do us any good.

Please use your influence so I can hold my head up in the paint shop at Vauxhall Motors.

GREGORY RASPUTIN,
61 Buzzard Avenue, Luton.

The Independent Television Authority,
Brompton Road, London S.W.3.

Gentlemen,

It would greatly assist our work as clinicians if you would instruct the TV companies under your control to ban the more sensational works of the writer Robert Louis Stevenson. It is truly said that television is seen by millions and there are times when this has an unfortunate effect. We do not ask you to ban all "doctor" plays and serials, indeed these help the status and

131

glamour of our calling. Our principal objection is naturally to television adaptations of "Dr. Jekyll and Mr. Hyde."

For months after any showing of this work our patients are in a difficult mood, and there have even been occasions when patients arriving too late for my morning clinic ask Reception to put them onto Mr. Hyde's afternoon list, under the impression they will actually be seeing the same man. This is particularly unfortunate if the error is not detected, as I specialise in skin conditions whereas Mr. Hyde mostly does circumsions.

I can assure you we are definitely two separate people, who are paid separate salaries by the hospital board.

> Yours faithfully,
> HENRY JEKYLL, M.D.
> EDWARD HYDE, CH.B.
> Queen Sophia's Hospital.
> London W.C.2.

The Managing Director,
Twentieth Century Fox Film Co. Ltd.

Dear Sir,

As your company together with several others has been responsible for the distribution of films incorporating my name in their titles, to my great embarrassment and inconvenience, I am writing to draw your attention to the fact that I am being driven to take legal action.

My wife, Lady Frankenstein, has been distressed by catcalling from groups of village women, and has on several occasions been greeted by ironic singing of "Here Comes The Bride." I myself have been approached more than once by locals who have combed their hair forward and adopted an idiotic clumping walk, while holding a pair of cider bottle stoppers to their temples to represent electrodes. These incidents have occurred usually after performances of films in the picture house at the local town, or so I have been told. I don't normally go myself.

I realise you wish to bolster up falling revenues with more films in the horror idiom but I warn you that if you plan to exhibit any of the group of films which use my name I shall sue.

> Yours faithfully,
> FRANKENSTEIN, M.F.H.
> The Manor House,
> Lower Sodding, Somerset.

"Darwin says 'ere, that all your life forms started in the sea . . .

. . . Then they slowly evolved, see. That makes all the livin' creatures one big family.

By the 'eck, Sid, just think, it were probably winkles like these that started it all."

"So that's your bloody game, well, I'm not 'aving your damn relatives livin' here."

HUMPHREY LYTTELTON

Waxing Nostalgic

In 1941, Duke Ellington collaborated with his son Mercer in writing a tune which they called "Things ain't what they used to be." Three years later, feeling perhaps that forty-five was a dangerous early age for grouchy retrospection, the Duke tried to change the name to "Time's a-Wastin'." Alas, the new forward-looking, go-getting, finger-snapping title didn't "take," as the medical saying goes. And that's why "Things ain't what they used to be" sticks out to this day like a glumly nostalgic sore thumb in the repertoire of the youngest and most optimistic seventy-one-year-old in the business.

The episode cannot have surprised him too much. Duke Ellington likes to put things in terms of "percentages," and no one knows better than he that over the great mass of mankind musical appreciation equals ten per cent intellectual comprehension, ten per cent physical response and eighty per cent nostalgia. Challenged once with playing too many old and familiar pieces in his concert programme, he explained "We have people in our audience who romanced and married to 'Mood Indigo,' and we're there for the purpose of making them happy." For Mood Indigo read "In a Monastery Garden," "Nellie Dean," Beethoven's Fifth, "Your Tiny Hand is Frozen" or "When the Saints Go Marching In" and you have the key to perennial popularity in music.

There are several deep-rooted misconceptions about nostalgia. One is that, like some other diseases, it has a long incubation period, withholding its familiar symptoms—the lump in the throat, the cold shivers, the involuntary watering of the eye—until the sufferer is advanced in life and reminded of his distant youth. This theory would certainly explain why old tunes keep coming back. It would do nothing to explain how they ever arrived in the first place. The fact is that nostalgia is practically instantaneous. Given a sufficiently powerful initial experience, it is possible for a subject to start waxing nostalgic within a few minutes. I have positive proof of this in the letters I receive after my weekly jazz record programme on the BBC. Each week more than one listener writes rapturously about some piece of music which I have just played. From the post-mark it is clear that he has written and posted the letter while the programme is still going on, implying a pretty hefty initial experience. The fact that he asks with great urgency how he can obtain the record shows that nostalgia has already set in. And nostalgia, like wine and cheese, matures with age. By the time he gets my reply and orders and receives the record from his local record

shop—a combined process that will take weeks rather than days—he will have worked up a kingsize nostalgia that is both chronic and incurable.

It's important here to scotch another popular misconception about nostalgia in music. Romantic circumstances may well enhance the occasion and heighten the susceptibilities, but they are not the prerequisite of nostalgia. With the deepest respect to Duke Ellington, it can safely be assumed that for every person who romanced and married to "Mood Indigo" there are a dozen who were cutting their toenails or sipping a solitary beer when they first heard the tune, and who will applaud its opening strains just as rapturously. Indeed, my experience of playing to Saturday night dancers in varying stages of the mating process has taught me that there is no audience less receptive than the young man who is engrossed in nibbling his girl-friend's ear—unless it be the lady herself whose wavelength is jammed, so to speak, by heavy breathing and hoarse whispers of endearment.

Having established that nostalgia in music is both instant and built-in, let's go on to tackle the belief that nostalgia, like a bee, can only sting once. Recent events in popular music have refuted the notion that a style of music, having once captivated a generation and coloured an era, then loses its powers of attraction and becomes simply period. In the 'Fifties, we had a Dixieland revival, during which young people born during World War II responded with deep nostalgic affection to a musical style and repertoire which in all probability brought their grandparents together just after World War I. The hairy and be-sweatered Traddy in 1955 who pounded the floor to the strains of trumpet, clarinet and trombone, knew and cared nothing of the Jazz Age, of Scott Fitzgerald or Paul Whiteman or the Original Dixieland Jazz Band. The sound of the banjo stirred in him some primeval urge to shimmy like his sister Kate and he reacted accordingly.

We have a perfect contemporary example of the power of music to induce nostalgia over and over again in the current—and by no means first—epidemic of Glenn

"I like a dictatorship. It limits the things one has to talk about."

134

"The truth is officer, I had been hoping to inherit the earth."

Milleritis. Musicians who earn their living faithfully reproducing the Glenn Miller sound of the 'Forties will confirm that a high proportion of their audiences are youngsters not old enough even to have been conceived to the strains of "Moonlight Serenade." There's no mystery to this. It just so happens that the sound of clarinet and saxophones blended together in syrupy harmony has a high nostalgia-factor regardless of whether it is associated with air-raid shelters, doodlebugs and reconstituted egg or with discotheques, jumbo jets and Wimpy bars.

For a composer or performer with an eye on mass popularity and royalties beyond the grave, this high nostalgia-factor is indispensable. Like many indispensables, it is also intangible. Beethoven hit it in several of his symphonies but in none of his Quartets. The Mills Brothers had it, the Ink Spots lost it in a welt of absurd mannerisms. Tchaikovsky could have done with a little less, Brahms with a little more. Gracie Fields got it without really trying, Jessie Matthews missed it by trying too hard. Glenn Miller, traditional jazz, Billie Holiday, the concertina, George Formby and Fats Waller have it in the bag, while Stan Kenton, ragtime, Ella Fitzgerald, the accordion, Will Fyffe and Charlie Kunz look like missing the bus.

When it comes to the mechanical side of popular music, we find that old wind-up gramophones have it in abundance, but the radiogram never made it. And I know from the way in which my correspondents refer in reverential terms to "78s," as though the numbers denoted a rare vintage rather than a technical specification, that those dear old crumbling, black digestive biscuits have a headstart which LPs, with all their posh covers, will never make up. The reason is that 78s handed us our nostalgia in palatable portions, three minutes at a time, and then left us alone until the next month's issue to digest it. And nostalgiawise, there was a lot to be said for being breakable and accident-prone. One record which I treasure in my memory far more dearly than its musical content deserves is "Blue Lou" by Errol Garner. I left it on a hot plate and inadvertently switched on. When I next saw her, Blue Lou was drooping over the edge of the hotplate like a Salvador Dali time-piece, never to speak again. They'll probably bring it out on LP, but it won't be the same.

In Praise of
Heartless Jokes

Kenneth Allsop's one man society for the encouragement of cruelty to people

I was in a taxi going along Wimpole Street the other day, and I noticed three shaggy students (two males and one female) huddled on the pavement against a house's iron railings, intent upon a hidden task. As I drew level, they finished and strode away with contented expressions of fulfilment such as usually dwell on the faces of only divines and gluttons. I saw that they had lashed to the spikes a lidless Bird's Custard Powder tin, and under it attached a notice in block capitals: CUSTARD'S LAST STAND.

That was time well spent, worth every moment away from their textbooks and essays. Everyone should put aside part of the day for japes, jests, tomfoolery and merry pranks, but with one proviso. Pleasant trifle thought it was which those banterers of Wimpole Street had conceived, it typically lacked bite. Humour is becoming slack and kindly, in fact good-humoured. Useless. To make practical jokes memorable you have to go for the jugular. Most people (even secret addicts and practitioners) get shifty about speaking out openly for pitilessly cruel jokes, so it becomes incumbent upon me to condemn the decadent, soft-hearted drollery being pat-a-caked about like blobs of dough. There's no room for sportsmanship. In this gladatorial arena sur matches cunning and malevolence with cur.

To be entitled to the reputation of practical joker you cannot pull your punches. Every heartless trick must be dirty and aimed low. You have to recognise the crucial psychological moment when your victim is most defenceless and relaxed, then thrust to destroy.

I have always found that children, being smaller, weaker and, with pathetic innocence, expecting fair play from adults, eminently vulnerable and satisfactory targets. My own are now getting too alert and muscular to fool with safety, but I still manage a reasonable amount of long-distance torment. For instance, I have now succeeded in getting three request records, each

with a different mawkish message, played for my younger son. His musical taste is for such underground groups as The Grateful Dead and Captain Beefheart. My three choices, carefully spaced, were for records by Rolf Harris, Val Doonican, and the latest Bobby Goldsboro, "Watching Scotty Grow." I think the last probably came as the most cutting whiplash, as it was broadcast at a time of maximum embarrassment for him, at a week-end when at least one or two of his friends were likely to have that programme drooling on, and so spread the news around.

Wherever I am I keep a sharp eye open for sickening picture postcards, those in strong poster colours showing kittens tangled in balls of wool, or a puppy and a chick cradled in an open Easter egg. I maintain a steady flow of these to my daughter in her final year at university, with cheery greetings written with pencil in a backward sloping hand.

But let me define more exactly the three methods of causing extreme discomfort or fright in others. First, there is the one described above, the leisurely Chinese drip torture by which one toys with one's prey so that they never know quite when next you will strike. One must stay vigilant for the random opportunity. For instance, I was delighted to spot on a rack a new paperback entitled *Bidding For Beginners*, which I sent to my brother-in-law, who is a bridge player of championship standard. Jean, the wife of my old friend David Malbert, with her own wheel and kiln, whose wares are eagerly bought. So it was immensely pleasing at a secondhand bookstall to come upon a slim volume, set in big square type, entitled *Simple Steps to Becoming a Potter*, with faded photographs of ladies with buns and in dirndl skirts kneading warped vessels. This I sent to Jean inscribed: "I am delighted to hear that you have taken up this little hobby. I am certain you will find it takes your mind off things."

The objective is a grinding erosion of confidence, repeatedly pulling the rug from under people. Distinguished operators of this technique are two TV film men I sometimes work with. The cameraman's nickname is Little Big Horn, partly because of his Custer-like (not custard-like in this case) resistance to almost any request or suggestion for a shot put to him by the director or reporter, but not for that reason alone. The sound-recordist is known as Trade Winds. All sound recordists are chronic acoustical neurotics whose tape machines overheat if a grasshopper's rasp intrudes, who are in eternal unattainable quest for perfect halcyon conditions. This particular chap has borne his name since, in the middle of a football field on a tropic island, no airline route within miles, not even a tree nearby to rustle while I recorded my commentary, he muttered querulously about the trade winds being in the wrong quarter. Little Big Horn and Trade Winds gang-up on the reporter or director, trying to break his nerve by constant quiet conversational comparisons with the skill of other reporters or directors, and expressing grave misgivings about the feasibility of an assignment in such hands as these. They have been known to make hardened war correspondents whimper and cry. The only defence is attack, and one has to wait for their first slip and ruthlessly pounce. On this particular trip by the greatest of good fortune Trade Winds accidently wiped a spool of tape, and Little Big Horn edge-fogged four hundred feet of exposed film by opening the wrong

tin, so the knives were permanently positioned between their ribs, and could easily be given a quick twist, either in retaliation or to scare them off if they started prowling round a situation sniffing spilled blood.

The second method is that of the puff adder, the instantaneous seizure of an unexpected opportunity, such as that made by an American columnist who, answering his telephone to hear someone with a wrong number ask for Barbara, with hesitation growled in a rough Hoboken voice: "Look, mac, I've moved in here now, so quit pestering Barbara, yunnerstan?" and put down the receiver. I feel that only recently I quite honourably rose to a chance of this kind. I was travelling up to London on a Monday morning with a couple who had been spending the week-end with me in the West Country. We got into an empty compartment; they took the seats adjoining the corridor and I slumped into a window seat and dozed. Several stops later we had been joined by two City gents and a rather frail middle-aged lady, and the air was getting stuffy. My friend rose and said, in general, "Do you mind if we have the window open an inch or two?" and, threading through the legs, jerked it down. It occurred to me that it would not be apparent to the other three travellers that we knew each other, so I sprang from the cushion and said in a loud hectoring voice: "Yes, you impertinent young swine, I *do* mind, so you'd better get that window closed, fast."

The paralysed shock which went quivering around

"*I don't mind him having affairs but he's so blatant about it.*"

"Now can we start a family?"

the group was most gratifying. It was beautifully exploited by my friend, who quick-wittedly got the idea, and sneered: "One more word from you, dad, and you'll be out of it." As he returned to his seat, I sent a mad laugh following him between the three pairs of nervously darting eyes and cried: "I'd like to see you try it!" I believe the letter in the *Daily Telegraph* a couple of days later, about the alarming increase in gratuitous violence in modern society, was referring directly to this incident.

The third method is that of elaborately structured Byzantine horseplay, which really requires a private income and the dedication of a metaphysical poet—the kind of planning and consultation which went into the fixing of Alexander Woollcott, who put the word around that he wanted the twelve-volume Oxford Dictionary for Christmas, so that twelve of his friends each presented him with Volume 1.

I have occasionally gone to time and trouble on this scale, such as when in hospital during the war, and after medical discharge, I received an official communication from the RAF in which had inadvertently been folded up a plain sheet of headed writing paper. One of my best friends in the ward had been a rear gunner on Whitley bombers. Grounded by a shrapnel wound in the knee, he never ceased to exult in his marvellous luck and to describe the terror and abomination in which he had held flying. I actually invented the Catch-22 device. I used the virgin sheet of Air Ministry paper to write to my friend, notifying him that as a result of a revision in regulations, he was being recalled

immediately to operational duties. He was, the letter informed him, posted forthwith to an East Anglian squadron renowned for its bleak desolation, the insane press-on aggressive policy of its CO, and its appalling losses. I hate to admit now than an hour after lights out, hearing his groans through the darkness, I released him from his agony.

But, although I am an advocate of the purging and purifying effect of the heartless joke, I cannot claim to be in the league of the sabre-toothed tigers of the craft—such as Woollcott himself and the great James Moran.

Woollcott was the kind of man who, when a close friend gave his name as a reference for his daughter's application to an exclusive, fashionable school, wrote to the headmistress: "I implore you to accept this unfortunate child and remove her from her shocking environment." S. N. Behrman made the same mistake when putting in for an apartment in a new block. In reply to the property company's inquiry about Behrman, Woollcott expressed amazement that they were considering as a tenant "such a notorious drunkard, bankrupt and all-round moral leper." Moran, an American philosopher and thoughtful japer, when on his way to a dinner party in Beverly Hills, on an impulse hooked a piece of string around his right ear, draped it down his cheek and into the corner of his mouth. As he moved from group to group, shaking hands and chatting, people at first stared raptly, then quickly averted their eyes, and made no mention of it, although Moran could hear around him whispered urgent discussions. No one spoke to him about the

string. From then on, for years, on air trips and on trains, Moran would often wear his string, calmly reading while pleasurably aware of the stir and speculation around him.

Another American, a publisher, has an admirably professional approach to offending people. He carries a supply of specially printed cards, each in a small envelope, and when he sees someone he knows in a restaurant or club he tips a waiter to take one across. The card reads: "The management request that you and your party leave quietly."

But, finally, it is not so much the elegantly scenarioed plot which causes emotional disturbance as inspired spontaneity. It is difficult to imagine a more ripely perfect joke, expertly roasting innate human decency on the spit, than that thought up at the last moment by an undergraduate whose college was entertaining young women at a dance. A three-department lavatory was set aside for the guests and labelled LADIES.

The youthful genius ripped into town, bought three goldfish at the pet shop and released one in each pan.

All evening girls were going through the door and retreating baffled. Not one could bring herself to disturb the goldfish. It is reported that as the night grew longer, the girls seemed to get livelier and livelier.

"I wish a mountie could get his woman now and again."

"I'm fed up with being a nuclear family, we should be living in a commune!"

CHILD POWER
BY HEATH

"Did you plan it, or goof it?"

"Oh, don't come the old 'you're not too old to be spanked' unk! You lack authority and you've always lacked authority!"

"I'd have left home years ago—but my parents need me around to hold the marriage together."

"Can you imagine what it will be like in a few years' time— I'll be slopping around the house full of pills, and you'll be wondering where you went wrong, plus the fact that we won't be able to communicate . . ."

"Look, you need me as much as I need you, so let's neither of us rock the boat too much."

"Listen mate! I didn't ask to be born but since you brought me into this mess the least you can do is stuff me full of sweets."

"THE LORD HATH COME!"

HAIFA HILTON

REGISTER

S. McMURTROX.

A View from the Peer

*LORD MANCROFT
on the advantages of not being
Mr. Mancroft*

On Friday 10 July, a dreadful thing happened to me. I opened my post and found that I had been sent a three-line Whip. I was bewildered and hurt. I have been a member of the House of Lords for nearly thirty years, and nobody has ever done such a thing to me before. Two lines; well, so be it. But three! What next?

It has now become clear what's next, and very disturbing it is, too. Owing to the creation of a large number of Life Peers the normal attendance in the Lords has been steadily and significantly increasing. We have had to put a lot more armchairs in the library, and the list of speakers for debates has become so lengthy that you can no longer get up after tea and begin your speech with those poignant words, "My Lords, at this late hour . . ."

This also means that at any moment the Government may be faced with a snap division, and if we get caught out and lose an important amendment, or worse still the Second Reading of a Bill, we're not going to endear ourselves to our colleagues in the Commons, and the next round of talks about Lords Reform will begin on quite a sour note.

Some members feel that we have now lost one of the great advantages that a Peer possesses, namely, the right to tell the Chief Whip what he can do with it.

The other advantages of being a Peer are of course pretty generally recognised. The House of Lords is the finest Club in the world: its demeanour is civilised and urbane, the Club premises are fine, the rules are sensible, and the service superb. Disraeli once remarked that the House of Lords reminded him of a ducal residence with his Grace lying dead in an upper chamber, but although the Lords is hardly the place to go for kicks, Dizzy was, I think, exaggerating. And there's no denying that there's less chance of having a C.S. gas-bomb lobbed at you in the Lords than there is down the Corridor in the Commons.

A title also helps you to get tickets for the theatre, or a table at the Savoy, but you have to tip disproportionately well in return. And at the rate of redemption current in most West End cloakrooms my umbrellas must now cost me about £25 each. Bankers and tailors are also beguiled by a title, but your overdraft and your overcoat will probably cost you more. And when the Playboat Club opened up in Park Lane, nearly every Peer of my acquaintance was invited to apply for membership, not to mention my Uncle Charlie who's been dead for many years.

A title is, however, a mixed blessing when travelling abroad. Some foreign porters and taxi-drivers seem to be impressed. Americans, on the other hand, probably

because their jazz musicians tend to have names like Count Basie, Earl Hines and Duke Ellington, are understandably puzzled.

I was once invited to address the Alabama branch of the English Speaking Union on the role of the House of Lords in our Constitution. I touched lightly on Magna Carta and the Petition of Rights. I explained in greater detail the relationship between the Executive and the Legislature, and drew a nice distinction between a Private Bill and a Private Member's Bill. I performed the same service for the Lord Chamberlain and the Lord Great Chamberlain. I also, I'm ashamed to say, indulged in flippancy at the expense of the Judicial Committee of the Privy Council.

I was listened to in stunned silence, and this continued well into question time. Eventually, to ease the embarrassment, the caretaker of the hall rose helpfully to his feet. "Why," he asked, "is the daughter-in-law of a dook called Lady Geroge Whatsit? She ain't a fella, is she?" You can't really blame the Americans for being confused, and it is as well therefore to be in a position to explain, among other things, why Miss Raine McCorquodale, Mrs. Gerald Legge, Viscountess Lewisham, and the Countess of Dartmouth have all been the same pretty person.

In Japan it's worse. What's more, the Japs used to have titles themselves, and therefore ought to know better. "You have a reservation for me?" I enquired at my Tokyo hotel, "Lord Mancroft?" "Ah, yes, Mr. Lord," they replied, bowing low, "one moment, please." "No, no," I said, seeing disaster looming, "Lord is not my name, it's only a title—but it really doesn't matter. Not to worry at all." "Ah, yes, Mr. Title," they said, beaming, happily, "we understand of course. So sorry. This way, please."

In some countries, therefore, titled travellers might be well advised to abandon their titles temporarily, and adopt a nom de voyage. Even so, they should always remember to ask for letters under the names of Mr. Lord, Mr. Bart, Mr. Rev, and Mr. Esq, as well as under their own.

These, however, are only minor disadvantages, and happily for some the major disadvantage of having a peerage has now been done away with. Until recently you could not sit in the Commons if you had become a Lord, or sit in the Lords if you were born a Lady. Both these biological handicaps have now been put to rights, and the repercussions have been less convulsive than was feared. There remains, then, the problem of the three-line Whip.

Shortly after I had signed the Roll, and taken my seat for the first time in the Lords, the division bells began to ring. I thought it would be a good idea to find out what we were supposed to be voting for. (I naturally had all that sort of nonsense knocked out of me as soon as I was appointed a Junior Minister.) So I went up

timidly to a character of majestic mien who was standing by the fireplace (I took him to be one of our Nobler Dukes, or at least a Scottish Representative Peer). "Sir," I said, "may I enquire what we are voting for?" "My Lord," he replied, "I am only the chap who fills up the coal scuttles. But since you've been good enough

"*Mummy can't bring you a magazine now. Mummy is busy serving lunch.*"

to ask my advice, let me give it to you. Never ask what you're voting for. Ask whom you're voting against."

That, I believe, is the nicest thing about being a Peer. In the long run you're beholden to nothing but your own conscience, though it is, of course, inadvisable to go for a long run too often.

As well as being the best Club, the House of Lords is also the finest Senate in the world. I am very proud to be a member of it, and I would not wish it otherwise. It can throw up an expert on every imaginable subject who only talks if he or she has something useful to say. We can debate wide-ranging subjects for which the Commons can't find immediate time. The debates are good though not always quite as good as we like to tell ourselves they are. This is not the only reason they are ill-reported in the press, but rather because public interest is and must be in the Commons. Politics is about Power, and it is in the Commons that Power lies.

We can revise untidy legislation and initiate our own. We can ultimately put a brake on dictatorship. But none of this can dispel a sense of frustration and impotence, or counteract the feeling of political make-believe that has been at the back of most attempts at Lords Reform.

Now, accidentally, the three-line Whip brings new life to the Lords. We may even start to matter. Whether this will prove an advantage remains to be seen. It will be seen by the first Noble and Tory Lord who lingers too long over the Cockburn '27, and, finding himself locked out of the Lobby, accidentally brings down the Government.

Sheridan's friend, Lord Bayforth, refused to leave White's for a Motion standing in his own name on the Order Paper until he had finished his second bottle of port, and the Lords waited patiently for him. When he did eventually turn up I'm sorry to say he was drunk.

The Lords, of course, have now changed in this respect as in others, though nobody has ever seemed quite clear whether the expression "Drunk as a Lord" should be taken as a compliment, or an insult.

"We must wait for a wind—I do not wish to stand accused of unprovoked aggression."

COUNCIL WITH NOBS ON

BILL TIDY looks at the Squirearchy in local affairs

*"**There's** a chappie who values his job!"*

It's such a bore having them both on the council."

"I'm pushing you up the housing list as fast as I can, Benson. Please open the gates!"

Naturally I mustn't take all the credit for the 'under twelves' new adventure playground, but . . ."

"Prizes will be graciously presented by Councillor Fleetwood-Horrocks's fourth gardener."

Caption Competition:

A weekly contest in which readers are invited to supply up-to-date captions to some venerable cartoons.

"Course, it'll be better when we've got the curtains up."

G. Vincent of London, SW5

1927 caption—The One: *"Why not greyhound racing?"* The Other: *"That's an idea."*

"I can never understand the Wednesday Play."

S. Paterson of Hamilton, Lanarkshire

1928 caption—WHAT OUR TELEVISIONISTS MAY HAVE TO PUT UP WITH: Voice of Broadcasting Lecturer: *"Now I will run through the Lithuanian vowel sounds once again, and this time I want you to watch my lips closely."*

"Actually, I'm trying to give up smoking."

G. Hamill of Cambridge

1943 caption.—"Well, what are you staring at—haven't you seen a man in a top hat before?"

"Say what you like about King Kong, he's a tidy eater."

J. Hardy of London, EC

1933 caption.—*"Lumme, Joe! I s'pose that was the 'ouse?"*

146

That Christmas and Elsie

By HARRY SECOMBE

" now for the news. Those who are squeamish about news may like to switch off at this point."

It was Christmas Day and I was fourteen and suffering from a severe attack of puberty.

"Silent Night . . ." I sang, head held slightly forward to catch the ray of winter sunlight coming through the stained-glass window above the altar. Elsie Thomas was in the front pew with her mother and I wanted to catch her eye. "Aaa-meen," I intoned loudly, trying to catch her ear as well.

The choirmaster glared at me in the mirror over the organ keyboard. My voice was breaking and the previous Sunday it had cracked in the seven-fold Amen.

"If I want yodelling I'll ask for it," he had said. "This is Swansea, not the Swiss Alps."

Now I blushed back at him in the mirror and knelt piously on my hassock, wearing my "Mickey Rooney as Andy Hardy being told off by his father" expression.

Elsie Thomas tittered and nudged her mother. The rest of the choir were sitting back comfortably waiting for the sermon to start, hard-boiled sweets already bulging in cheeks. I dropped my head and pretended a prayer while the Vicar said, "In the name of the Father and of the Son and of the Holy Ghost. Amen." I then rose gracefully and sat back in Arthur Williams's lap.

"Gerroff," he bleated, loudly enough to earn me another glare from the mirror and a further titter from Elsie.

I resumed my own seat and fumbled sweatily for a pear drop in my cassock pocket. Things weren't going as I had planned. I did a mental dissolve into the Church Social the week before when Elsie Thomas had swept into my life.

She was a new arrival in our midst, her family only recently coming down from one of the valleys north of the town. She was blonde and pretty and had the lads at the Social swarming around her in no time at all.

I kept aloof, though. Mildred Rogers had caught hold of my jacket.

"You go and join that lot around Elsie Thomas, and I'll tell my Mam you wanted to play 'Doctors and Nurses' in the coal house last Saturday." That stopped me. Mildred's mother used to carry her husband home under her arm from the pub on pay nights.

"I have no intention of going. Anyway I'm doing my impressions later on and I've got to go and rehearse."

I walked away towards the unheeded plates of sandwiches and stuffed myself. I listened to the boastful

chatter of the boys surrounding Elsie. Wait until I do my impressions, I thought.

The Vicar clapped his hands. "Take your seats please, our concert is about to begin."

There was a clattering of chairs and faces all turned towards the little stage. I took up my position behind the two draped blankets which acted as curtains.

"First we have Master Harry Secombe who is going to give us a comedy turn. Master Harry Secombe." The Vicar waved a plump hand and the blankets jerked slowly back.

"Hello folks," I said nervously, my lips cleaving to my gums, revealing my teeth in a macabre grin. Laughter immediately rang out. Tinkling laughter from Elsie Thomas. "Ooh, there's funny."

I went into my impression routine. Stainless Stephen, Sandy Powell, Lionel Barrymore could hardly be heard for Elsie's continuous laughter. The others joined in, not really knowing why, because after all I had done the same turn at Church Socials dozens of times. But Elsie's laughter was infectious. I was so elated by my reception that I even gave an impression of our milkman, which was a mistake as he was sitting in the third row.

Then I swaggered back down into the audience.

"There's funny you are," said Elsie giggling.

"Hush!" said Mildred Rogers, "the Curate's tap-dancing." She looked furious.

I turned to Elsie and did my "Mickey Rooney meets Anne Rutherford for the first time" look.

"I'm Harry Secombe."

She burst out laughing again. Someone hit me heavily behind the left ear.

"A bit of order for the Curate," said our milkman, smirking.

Elsie was now stuffing a handkerchief in her mouth, and tears were running down her face. I could see

"*It was nature's way of slowing him down.*"

Mildred's mother making her way stealthily towards us.

"I'll see you tomorrow night at the top of Morris Lane after choir practice. Half-past seven." She nodded, gurgling away into her hanky.

I reached the door of the hall just before Mildred's Mam did.

"What's this about you operating on our Mildred?" was all I heard before I shut the door.

All next day in school I was in a happy daze, although no one noticed. My attitude towards learning was one of perpetual bewilderment only paralleled by the despair of those who had the task of teaching me. I took three years to make a wire dish mop in metal-work class. When I took it home my mother thought it was a clothes brush.

As soon as I saw Elsie that night she started to laugh. I hadn't even spoken a word, but she was off. She didn't even notice I was wearing my father's grey trilby and my brother's off-white mac with only two buttons missing and a slightly torn pocket.

I walked alongside her in silence until she had settled down a bit.

"Will you be my girl friend?" I was wasting no time in asking her. That set her off again.

"Ooh dear, stop it," she gasped, clutching a lamp-post for support. "I've got a stitch, take me home."

We had only been together about five minutes, but there was nothing else to do. As we passed Mildred's house her mother was at the gate. Elsie was still laughing and holding herself.

"Oh yes," said Mrs. Rogers, "using laughing gas to operate now, are you doctor?"

I pulled my hat further over my eyes and took the helpless Elsie to her front door.

"See you in Church on Christmas Day, I'm singing a solo in the Carol Service. You won't laugh then." I left her and walked home determined to show her the more serious side of my nature. After all laughter is not the only thing in life.

"Amen." I came back to the present quickly. The sermon was over and my big chance to impress Elsie was coming up fast . . . my solo. After this, and the pink sugar mouse I'd bought for her waiting in my overcoat in the vestry, she'd have the sort of adoring respect for me that Judy Garland had for Mickey Rooney in *Babes In Arms*.

The face in the mirror was glaring again. I gripped my carol book tightly and opened my mouth.

"Noel, Noel, Noel, No . . ." On the fourth "Noel" my voice disintegrated. It splintered into a thousand fragments. With it went my boyhood and before me lay a

"No, we don't reckon on having any more kids. I've decided to let the wife lie fallow for a while."

wilderness of pimples, spots and slow-growing hairs to be crossed before I could call myself a man.

I stopped and turned to the choirmaster pointing at my throat.

From the front pew Elsie's smothered laughs came in waves. Someone else took over the solo and all eyes went back to the books. Except Elsie's. Her mother was guiding her swiftly up the aisle towards the door, giving her little thumps on the back to try to stop her laughing.

That's it. Voice gone, girl gone. Then I thought of that pink sugar mouse in my overcoat pocket and my face began to stop burning. I wondered if Mildred was doing anything that night.

The Glorious Twelfth

By LORD ARRAN

Suddenly I am fashionable: I shoot grouse. In fact people have been shooting them for a hundred years or more but until recently nobody paid the slightest attention. I have also been shooting pheasants and partridges since my childhood, but for some reason that still doesn't count. The "grouse" image does.

I suppose it all started with Mr. Harold Macmillan, though the "grandson of a crofter," his favourite phrase, can hardly be described as "trendy." No one got in the least excited about say the Duke of Roxburghe, "Birdseye Bobo" to his friends, who has literally slain thousands, indeed tons of thousands of these off-black birds. All these years his achievements went as it were unnoticed. He was not on the map. There is no justice.

Of course it doesn't matter whether you shoot grouse well or badly—except that if you shoot as badly as I do nowadays you don't get asked at all. It is just that you shoot. To be booked on the night sleeper to Perth or Ripon or Aberdeen on the eleventh is in the eyes of the press to have arrived. Of course they are quite wrong: the birds don't fly well for the first week or so. They are equally wrong in talking of someone as having "bagged" so many birds—a word never used by those who shoot. But small matter.

What is not fashionable and indeed counts against you is to shoot someone else including a beater: publicity or failing publicity the gossip is positively damning.

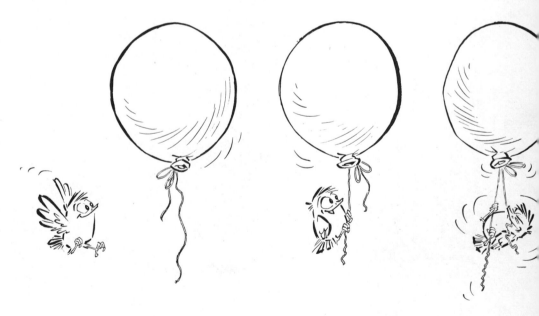

I was once shot by a Prime Minister in the hat, but as I pointed out in the case of Mr. Macmillan, a Prime Minister is a Prime Minister: not only does he set fashions but he can get away literally with murder. A Lord can't, so I take great trouble not to shoot anyone which is sometimes quite difficult in the confusion of the moment when the birds are coming thick and fast. Once I fired both barrels into the next-door butt thinking it empty. It was full. But so bad was my aim they didn't even notice.

Dog-shooting is also to be avoided. Only a royal host might dare it on the grounds that the animal was running in and spoiling the drive. But just as Crown Prince Rudolf's killing of Baroness Vetsera caused the Austrian throne to wobble, so Prince Philip could endanger the British monarchy if he shot Rover on the moors.

A warning shot may be fired across the bows of poachers and hikers but only discreetly and from not less than sixty yards. An alternative is to take out a wild beast, like a friend of mine who in successive years brought out a leopard, a tiger and a lion. The leopard was the most successful. Though it ate one in six of the birds it retrieved, it spread panic among those who were unlawfully on the beat. As its keeper said "they

"I believe they're planning an ancestral home to boost attendance figures."

gave an awful scream as it bounded after them." This is true. I only tell true stories.

Grouse are strange birds. Sometimes they're there: sometimes they're not. When they're not it is usually due to a wet, cold nesting season or overshooting which means there aren't enough left, or undershooting when they get disease, or inadaquate heather-burning, or even mass migration as ten years ago when the sky was dark with birds on their way from Aberdeenshire to Perthshire. When it's very hot, they are too lazy to get up; when it rains, again they also lie low. They are utterly unpredictable. Rarely do they come up to the journalists' cliché, "Birds were plentiful and strong on the wing."

Blood-sports may be wrong. I just don't know. It is a matter for each man's or woman's own conscience. I do know that there is nothing to compare with crouching in a butt, your loader alert beside you ready to throw you your second gun, his dog whining with excitement, three hundred yards ahead a covey with the wind under their tails. Will you get none: or one: or perhaps two, or even three? Will you even get your second gun off at all? Probably not if you're me.

Yes, grouse shooting is tremendously exciting and sometimes quite dangerous. It is also a political asset. Five at least of the thirty-four Tory majority can be claimed by Messrs. Purdey. Came polling-day, the voters, particularly in the northern constituencies, preferred grouse to Gannex. I don't blame them.

151

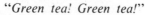

"Green tea! Green tea!"

"Give me one!"

What makes the Japanes

WILLIAM DAVIS, examines the Japanese funny-bone.

Just about the worst thing that can happen to you in Japan is to be caught with holes in your socks.

Japan is the land of the peek-a-boo feet, a part of the world where you spend your day stepping in and out of shoes. Davis-San would like to eat sashami? Right, let's have your shoes. A stroll around Kyoto's Nijo Castle? *Hai*, in your stockinged feet. A geisha party? OK, friend, off with your boots. To stay shod, when all around are discarding the trappings of Western civilisation, is as wicked as trying to hook the Emperor's sacred carp.

I've stripped down to my black, grey, and light-blue nylon socks on countless occasions, and I've felt faintly ridiculous every time. Deprived of their solid casing feet tend to look embarrassingly big. And there's always that nagging question: have they suffered from the heat? Shoes are as necessary to one's manhood as Cambodia is to Richard Nixon. Only the kinky enjoy being tickled by a two-inch splinter; I prefer to have thick leather between my tender sole and mother earth. If one has to strip, however, the first commandment is to check one's trendy hose for damage before setting out to explore the mysteries of the Orient. Greater tragedy hath not this world than a big, naked toe exposed to the penetrating gaze of a dozen giggling Japanese.

Not that they would actually giggle. Tokyo may be, in the words of my guidebook, "thrice as raucous as Chicago," but Japanese politeness is rightly proverbial. It is also practical. Most Japanese have a highly developed sense of self-status, and are intensely preoccupied with their public image. They try to dodge embarrassing situations, not just out of sympathy for the victims, but because they are reluctant to get involved. If you

152

laugh at someone, he may retaliate by getting a laugh out of you. Ridicule is disaster; the oriental obsession with "face" is one of the many things which distinguishes this supposedly Westernised nation from us. The insides of your fellow-guests may be twisted with laughter, but the outsides will pretend not to notice.

The elephant's sign says:
"I need another thirty minutes to get hungry."

"Please follow me."

"Sit down."

ugh?

Knowing this, of course, does not make one feel any better; I'd rather see everyone having a good laugh and getting it over with.

This unwillingness to get involved explains a lot of other things. It's the main reason why Westerners find the Japanese "inscrutable." The Japanese dislike having to give a straight answer to a straight question. It's a trait which they share with the communist countries. It makes them surprisingly indecisive, and averse to joining in any kind of public debate. A half-humorous maxim among white collar workers is "yasuma-zu, okure-zu, hatar-aka-zu"—don't be absent, don't be late, don't work. Many people hesitate to take their annual holiday for fear their superiors will discover how little they've been doing. Don't draw attention to yourself, and you'll be all right.

Add to this the well-publicised fact that the Japanese have a highly developed herd instinct, and that defeat and occupation produced an inferiority complex which has made it difficult for people to laugh at their country's foibles, and you realise why one hears a lot about Japan's so-called economic miracle, but nothing about Japanese humour.

Is there such a thing? Well, every country has its stock of jokes, and Japan is certainly no exception. There are several thriving humour magazines, and the more extrovert type of citizen gets as much pleasure out of circulating jokes as he does anywhere else. Most of them have a familiar ring. The editor of one monthly magazine, *Manga*, told me that a lot of his jokes are sent in by housewives, students, and hospital patients. Desert island jokes head the list, followed by quips about Ginza bar girls and spies. Hen-pecked husbands are another popular target and readers are fond of "pink" jokes—

sexy jokes. I asked him to translate a few gags which he considered particularly funny.

"Well," he said, "there's this one about a group of cannibals. Today, says one of them, it's the first time we've had reason to be thankful to God. We've just eaten the missionary.

"And this one about a young husband, whose mother telephones him in the middle of the night. It's me, mama, she says. Happy birthday.

"The young man—just twenty-two—is understandably surprised. Thank you, he says. But why wake me up at 2 a.m.?

"Because, the mother says, you did the same to me twenty-two years ago."

The Editor's two companions laughed uproariously; he had obviously hit his mark. But, of course, this isn't Japanese humour—it's the kind of stuff which you are just as likely to hear in Britain, Russia, Germany and, for all I know, Peking. It would be unfair to conclude that Douglas McArthur was right when he said that Japan was a nation of twelve-year-olds. It is, nevertheless, true that what makes most Japanese laugh is very different from the abrasive, sophisticated, often sick

humour one hears so much in the United States. Jokes about cannibals and spies have one great virtue: they don't really offend anyone.

Cartoons are, for the most part, in the same vein. There's the ubiquitous desert island (girl to boy: "don't tell anyone about us") and an assortment of gags about mice, spies, and elephants. There are jokes about harmless Japanese traditions like the tea ceremony, and a great many "pink" gags. There are cartoons either taken directly from American journals (and from *Punch*) or drawn in the style of well-known Western artists. The Western influence is strong, especially on the young. Apart from magazines, the Japanese also see a great deal of Western television. On one day during my latest stay Tokyo's twelve channels carried Ironside, Ben Casey, the Lone Ranger, I Love Lucy and the Adventures of Rin-Tin-Tin. (You haven't lived until you've heard Lucy throwing tantrums in Japan-

ese.) My Fair Lady was a smash-hit in Japan; so was Annie Get Your Gun.

What is missing, despite this influence, is the kind of hard-hitting political cartoon one sees in Britain and America. Humour is used to entertain; satire, the cruel part of humour, hardly seems to exist. The one newspaper cartoonist of note draws spidery cartoons on page one of the Asahi Shimbum. He pokes fun at things like the Japanese obsession with cars. Husband and wife sit on the roof of a garage; the caption says "Now we'll have to buy a house."

The Japanese Government has little to fear. This isn't the fault of cartoonists—the ones I met said they felt frustrated—but of editors. The Japanese (at least the ones who wield power) are immensely nationalistic. They are determined to show western countries that they can be beaten at their own game. Ergo, there must be no mockery of national institutions. Later on, per-

154

haps, when the gross national product has climbed still further. But not now.

Some of the people I talked to thought there were already signs of change. One Western ambassador told me that economic success had brought a greater degree of self-assurance, and that this was gradually making the Japanese more willing to laugh at themselves. The old order was breaking down; the young, particularly, were in "a more unbuttoned mood than ever before." He felt that Expo provided evidence of this. A high-ranking Japanese official had told him that they had tried to create "the fabulous and the absurd." There was, for example, the Tower of the Sun, which had the sun-goddess leering, at the opening of the ceremony, over the shoulder of the Emperor and the whole Japanese establishment. This would have been quite unthinkable thirty years ago, when the Emperor was considered the son of the goddess.

This, clearly, is the kind of thing which impresses the Japanese more than it does the Western eye. And it highlights one of the difficulties involved in trying to analyse another country's humour; one has to be Japanese before one can really hope to understand all the subtleties. The fact remains, nevertheless, that public mockery of national institutions is still comparatively rare. Ministers have an easy run, and no one ever mocks the Emperor. Even the gross national product is relatively safe. (Though I'm happy to say that, in private conversation, one Japanese friend referred to it as "Gross National Pollution.") The one exception—and it's an interesting one—is the military machine.

Young and old have so thoroughly rejected militarism, in favour of commercial aggressiveness, that the hero of yesteryear—the samurai—is a major figure of fun. A television programme called Geba-Geba, which is the Japanese equivalent of Laugh-In, invariably makes him its favourite target. So do many cartoonists. A recent issue of *Manga* carried a drawing of Osaka Castle, built by the fierce Japanese ruler, General Hideyoshi. It shows him emerging from the castle entrance, samurai sword in hand, and shouting to the assembled organisers of Expo: "Quiet please!"

American and Russian militarism also attracts attention, but by Western standards the attack seems mild. The Japanese both respect and resent the Americans. This is partly a hangover from the occupation, and partly the result of a genuine admiration for US economic strength. Newspapers, businessmen and politicians are, however, more reluctant to give voice to resentment in public than the students—or, indeed, than cartoonists in the United States itself.

As in every country, of course, there are individuals who defy generalisations. In three lengthy visits to Japan I have met many individuals with a keen sense of humour. Soichiro Honda, for example. I spent a highly entertaining afternoon with him at his experi-

"*This is the way to squeeze the hi-jackers.*"

mental workshop on the outskirts of Tokyo. A small man, with rosy cheeks, a healthy tan, and a mouthful of gold teeth, he is the antithesis of the big tycoon image. He knocked on the door of his small reception room and appeared, cap in hand, in greasy overalls. He made fun of the pretentiousness of fellow-tycoons, and laughed uproariously at his own jokes. He said he never went near his presidential suite at Honda head office because it was "such an uncomfortable place." As a young man,

155

he was dismissed from his technical high school "and if I had to take the exams set by my own company, I wouldn't pass." He had no time for leisure "because the fellows here are such slave-drivers" (laugh) and his nightlife was "in the hands of Mrs. Honda" (laugh). We drank nothing stronger than tea during our long conversation. Experience has taught me, however, that the best way to discover what makes a Japanese laugh is to get him drunk.

The Japanese are great drinkers. Like the Russians, they have no idea when to stop. While sober, they are generally serious and reserved. When drunk, they throw off all their reserve. A drunken Japanese is the happiest, most boisterous man alive. He sings, he dances, he tells jokes, and he plays silly games. No party is considered a success until all the participants are thoroughly stoned.

My first geisha party was considered an unqualified success. The sake was plentiful, and the geishas expensive. It started slowly, but warmed up fast. An hour later, I'd even forgotten about my shoes. And not for the reasons you think. For one thing, the Geishas weren't dressed for it. Mine wore a heavy kimono, her wig was done up in classic "gingko leaf" style, and her face was covered with a thick coat of clown-white make-up consisting, I was informed, of liquid powder and face cream. No, my forgetfulness was due to non-stop sips of sake, and to the realisation that, if I ever wanted to get to know the Japanese, I'd have to forget about dignity.

While she poured, my geisha chatted to me in Japanese. Geishas are experts in making a man feel witty, clever and altogether irresistible to the opposite sex. They smile, flatter, whisper. They tell you jokes, and listen to yours. They treat you as if you are the most fascinating chap on earth. They entertain with baleful samisen numbers, singkouta and nagauta songs, and execute slow-motion posture dances. Her jokes were, alas, wasted on me, but I gather they were very good. It didn't really matter. My hosts, a group of highly intelligent businessmen, were crawling about on all fours, and playing pat-a-cake and musical chairs—with sabuton cushions substituted for seats. Laugh? I thought we'd never stop.

It was all quite absurd—and very Japanese. It showed that, however Westernised many Japanese have become, they still live in a very different world. There are other features which serve the same purpose, notably some of Japan's off-beat industrial psychiatry. One company uses Madame Tussaud type mirrors which allow people with inferiority complexes to look like giants, and cut the arrogant down to size. Another has the President's face painted on punchbags, and invites employees to release their feelings of frustration. It couldn't happen anywhere else.

There is also a good deal of humour in Japanese literature. Most of the comic stories written over the centuries lack the spite one finds so often in ours. The emphasis is on entertainment; even in literature, the Japanese prefer to laugh together rather than at each other. (Practical jokes, incidentally, are almost unknown.) Because the Japanese language is eminently suited to word-play, literary humour tends to be subtle, often poetical. But it lacks nonsense as well as spite; there's nothing like "the Walrus and the Carpenter."

Japanese literature (and, no less important, Japanese caricature) merits a separate analysis. If you're interested, I strongly recommend the books of Dr. R. H. Blythe, published by the Hokuseido Press in Tokyo. Let me be content with a few examples.

I personally like the story about the thief who, discovered by the master of the house, was at a loss what to do. Unable to run away, he stood with his arms outstretched on the wall and said: "This is your shadow, Sir."

I'm also rather fond of the story, first published in 1730, about the new servant boy who was possessed by a fox. After prayers and exorcisms, he was dispossessed of it at last, but he seemed to be still absent-minded. The master got angry, and shouted: "You became a big fool since you were possessed by a fox!" The fox stuck his head in the window and said: "He was like that from the beginning!"

Not least, there is the story of the man—no genius—who went to his father-in-law's for the first time, determined to make a good impression. His friend said to him: "If you do not utter a single word you will be thought a fool, so say something, if only a greeting." "Yes, I quite understand." When he went there he was silent from the beginning to the end, but just as he was leaving he said to his father-in-law, "Have you ever seen a duck with arms?" "No, I haven't." "Nor have I."

Japanese or not, the story rings my chimes. So do some of Japan's more popular proverbs:

It's cheaper to buy than to receive a gift.

The samurai picks his teeth, even though he has not broken his fast.

Repeating the name of Buddha in a horse's ear. (Most of the art, music, and poetry of our world is little more than this.)

Killing the roots by straightening the branches.

The one who begins to talk about it is the one who farted.

A fan in autumn. (An unwanted, deserted woman.)

Monkeys laughing at the red bottoms of other monkeys.

I'll end on that. When we really know this, and still laugh at other red bottoms, it's true laughter. The Japanese may find it more difficult than their ancestors did to laugh at red bottoms. But are we really so much better?

⇩ 光
　線

JONATHAN MILLER was one of a select team of gifted amateurs handpicked as a service to the country to form the PUNCH SHADOW CABINET. His personal brief was to be Opposition Minister of Transport.

THE PUNCH SHADOW CABINET

I snatch at the portfolio for Transport, not out of any true interest in roads or rolling stock, but because I would enjoy the opportunity of making the motorist's life a misery. In case this sounds like idle pedestrian pique let me explain that my malice automatically excludes those who merely exploit the motor car in the pursuit of either profession or pleasure. The victim that I have in mind is the motorist *proper*—or to use his own cant phrase "the road user." The man, that is, who enthusiastically identifies himself with the fraternity of drivers, even when he is not actually behind the wheel of a car.

Happily for me, this fraternity already regards itself as embattled in some obscure way by petty officialdom; and usually refers to itself, on a collectively self-righteous note, as "the sorely tried motorist." In other words these are the folk who are motorists by positive moral conviction and for whom the pleasure given by the motor car is something much larger than the mere satisfaction which they derive from its mechanical and social convenience. These are the people who congregate in silently admiring knots whenever an exotic sports model parks seductively at the kerb; those for whom esoteric motoring accessories are de rigeur—chequered headlamp snoods, supernumerary rear lights, stringback gloves. So strong is their commitment to internal combustion that they advertise their devotion in the form of reflexive slogans stuck in the rear windows of their cars. "Cut Motor Taxes"; "I've got a Tiger in my Tank" and "Brands Hatch July '70." You never see fountain pens engraved with hortatory mottos on behalf of calligraphy; "Support Italic Hand"; "I've got a secretary Bird in my Barrel"; "Cut the Impôt on Inkpots Now."

The point is surely that for the rational mind, driving, like writing, has no subjective content over and above its mere accomplishment. Once it becomes an independent creed in its own right—that way madness lies.

It is interesting to note in this context that the hard core motorist is peculiarly given to the gummed sticker as a method of expressing all his other beliefs—beliefs, moreover, which are apparently independent of motor cars as such. Wherever you see such slogans as "Support Rhodesia"; "Keep politics out of Sport" or, as once, "Don't Blame me I voted Conservative" you can be sure that you are following someone who would think of himself as "a long suffering motorist." Does this mean then that motoring, as a creed, veers by additional conviction to the political Right?

This seems an odd assertion, but the fact is that there *is* a close affinity between motoring enthusiasm and reactionary opinion.

Why should this be? It arises, I believe, from some daft equivocations that exist in the right wing mind, in connection with the idea of individual freedom. Consider the true blue motorist's attitude to speed and its limits. For those who take motoring seriously, velocity has become a metaphor of rugged British individualism, and any attempt to clamp down on it, even in the name of safety, is regarded as an impudent infringement of personal liberty. Anyone with John Bull's red blood in his veins can race with safety; and as for the influence of alcohol, anyone who's man enough to drive in the first place is invariably improved with a tot inside him. Cry God for England, Mini and Nuits St. George! A fistful of Ale and Tankful of Tiger Juice and Heigh Ho for open road! To patriotic bravos of this stripe, it is no coincidence that the 70 m.p.h. speed limit and the breathalyser should both have been introduced by a non-driving woman socialist.

Just as the rednecks of the American Right agitate against restrictive firearm legislation by referring to the constitutional right of all citizens to bear arms, the British motorist or Mo-Tory, regards unlimited speed as his national birthright—something which was implied, even if not overtly expressed, in the small print of Magna Carta. Just think of the self-righteous fuss provoked by the introduction of the radar speed trap. Unsporting they said it was! Unsporting? There was no outcry on behalf of personal liberty when the radio telephone was used for the first time in the arrest of Crippen. Ban the Identikit! Preserve the freeborn Englishman's right to criminological anonymity! Keep the coppers on a par with John Q Public!

The point is that the Mo-Tory is completely inconsistent in his attitude to the privileges and equipment of the police. Hand in hand with a thorough-going permissiveness with respect to the ethics of the road goes an equally radical desire for retributive restraint as applied to the common criminal. The reintroduction of the rope will proceed apace with the abolition of the seat-belt. Small wonder then that Southern Africa features so strongly in the rear window rhetoric of such a group. It's the freeborn motorist's paradise, where you can tear up the roads at ninety, play cricket with the partners of your choice, down pint after pint of draught whisky at twopence a tot. How unlike the Old Country, rotted now both by permission and restraint!

These are the folks who I would hound, given the Ministry of Transport. How though? Who can say. I will do such things. What they are I know not, but they shall be the terror of the earth!

Quentin Blake

Square Measure

Trends?

They give me the bends,
And in divers directions
(Ha-ha, any objections
To one.
Small pun?),
Chiefly on account of their knack
Of keeping on coming back,
Though never in exactly the same form
As when they were last the smart, short-lived norm . . .
Though beards, e.g., are among current larks,
They don't come on Sheridan Morley the way they came on
   Karl Marx.

The trends' espousers
Are much ruled by trousers,
Whose main strength
Is all that piddling about with the width and length,
Which can also characterise
Ties,
Those that were string
In the Spring
And about as long
As a thong
Growing a mile wide
By Whitsuntide.

Or take shoulders:
One day as big as boulders,
Then suddenly sloping to the sleeves
Like eaves.

No wonder tailoring's stopped being bespoke,
By the time the latest style's cut and fitted it's a joke,
Whereas, off the peg,
You can at least find this week's arm and leg,
Though what happens to last week's stockpile is anyone's
   guess,
Probably dumped in Loch Ness.
One thing, the mad rush for the next styles
Is great for the boys in textiles,
There's a surefire boom
At the loom,
Whether they're backing
Jackets that used to be called hacking
(But this time the revers

Practically cover your ears)
Or whether
We've all got to go over to those Morecambe an
   double-breasters with the buttons set too close toge

And the lads who sell,
Whether it's the newest news in booze, fashionable ve
   the gracious domestic smell,
(Hell,
From the commercials you often can't tell)
Know perfectly well
That they'll ring the bell
Now that everybody equates mere newness
With U-ness.

And if that
Doesn't make me old hat——
Talking about things being U
Went out around 1962———
It brings me to the tiresome tintinnabulary
Of the trendy vocabulary.
Trendy. Even the word
Will soon sound absurd
Instead of deliciously heady . . .
Perhaps it's dead already.
You have to be wary:
Are they still calling things "hairy"?
Is "gear" still here?
When did "dig"
Stop going big?

The chap who remembers to say "groovy"
To prove he
'S on the ball
Proves he isn't at all.
You can get up-tight
(If that's still right)
Trying to show you're not a crumbling old freak
By talking a language that died last week.
Also by thinking a crew cut
Is still the new cut,
Or finally plunging into the wild thrills
Of shirts with frills
Just when everyone who matters
Is dropping them for fronts as plain as platters.

It's not much good trying to be with it,
Ith it?

Yet there's no doubt about it,
You hate being without it.

But, blast,
Things move so fast.
On Tuesday you're trendy,
And hopelessly dated on Wendy:
Another move to be non-U,
And a new U's on you.
You do your best,
Short of having "Stamp Out Reality" printed across your
    vest,
Or wearing so much hair
That nobody realises you're there,
But you're still going to be conscious of a lack
Until winkle-pickers come back
(They went out, the swine,
That week I bought mine).
Well, they could, you know, and with them, though the
    imagination sags,
Oxford bags,
The well-scrubbed look,
Reading the Good Book,
Hats,
Spats,
Honorificabilitudinity,
Virginity,
Calling fathers "Sir,"
And all the other things that aren't trendy at the moment but
    once were.

The trouble is that with me and you,
When they do,
We shall still find
We're panting behind,
Late starters with the electric guitar
When the young have chucked it for reciting extracts from
    that thing about Young Lochinvar.

You need youth,
And that's the truth,
To keep spot-on.
Without it—and it's a conclusion worth coming to if you
    have any feelings about how people of your age ought to
    behave and retain a modicum of respect all round—being
    trendy is simply not on.

BASIL BOOTHROYD

*"Good God!"—You're not wearing
your Hardy Amies to a demo?"*

161

KEITH WATERHOUSE presents

Marriage, you had better understand from the very beginning, is no joke. Those strip cartoons of domestic life, where the wife is always buying new hats or signalling a right-hand turn in order to dry her nail-varnish, and the husband is forever marooned in one corner of a newly-painted room, have as much to do with the real thing as your cheapskate engagement ring has to do with the Koh-i-noor diamond.

Married bliss is grim and married bliss is earnest, as you will find before you have even had time to tip the confetti out of your shoes. The problems facing two people about to live under the same roof, let alone share the same bed, are so complex and terrifying that even the kind of manual they send out in a plain wrapper prefers to gloss over them and distract the reader with unprintable euphemisms.

We will attempt to deal with some of these problems here, provided it is understood that we are merely skimming the top of the iceberg, and that Mr. and Mrs. Newlywed, sooner or later, will have to learn the hard way.

Making sucking noises

When the excitement of the honeymoon has worn off and you settle down to a lifetime of quiet evenings in front of the telly, it will slowly dawn on you that your partner is in the habit of making sucking noises, either through the medium of a hollow tooth or by introducing the tongue to the roof of the mouth.

There is nothing obscene or disgusting about this; indeed some Polynesian tribes do it all the time. But what is normal to one person may be distressing or even frightening to another. If these sucking noises are really getting on your nerves, and you are quite sure that they are not a reprisal for your own knuckle-cracking or whistling through the teeth, have a quiet word with your partner. Explain gently that if you had really wanted to spend night after night after night listening to a repertoire of barnyard imitations, you would have married an intelligent cocker spaniel.

Tensions in marriage

"Will I be able to satisfy her?" is supposedly the question that worries young bridegrooms most. What should worry them even more is, "Will she be able to find the end of the Sellotape after I have finished using it?" Nothing is more infuriating than a husband or wife who, having taken solemn vows before an ordained minister to make life as cushy as possible for the party of the second part, puts the Sellotape back in the right-hand drawer of the desk without folding the end bit back to save wear and tear of the other partner's nails. It is even more infuriating when the Sellotape is put back in the *left*-hand drawer of the desk, where even a child of four ought to know it does not belong.

Preparing for bed

Ringing the changes is what keeps a marriage fresh and interesting, and nowhere is this more important than in the approach to the marriage bed. If, at precisely eleven o'clock each night for fifteen years, you have been in the habit of stretching elaborately and announcing, "Ah, well, me for Bedfordshire," try surprising your partner with some new or daring variation. Say, "Ho, hum, me for beddy-byes."

Chewing pencils

If you chew pencils, so that whenever your partner wants to scribble a note to the milkman or to a lover, that partner is forced to handle what looks like a thin cylinder of ossified bacon-rind with a convention of

death-watch beetles going on inside it, you are asking for trouble. You are asking for even more trouble if you chew ballpoint pens.

Every kind of gratification may be accepted in marriage, *provided that it is acceptable to both sides*. Chewing pencils is not. Chewing pencils is a filthy perversion. As for chewing ball-point pens, people like you should be put away for life.

Telephone bills

In even the most deeply-satisfying partnership of minds and bodies, there may come a moment when one or other partner is arrested on suspicion of knocking the district nurse off her bicycle and interfering with her clothing. Or perhaps, God willing, the crisis may be of a more homely description: the eldest boy has been expelled for unspeakable practices behind the gymnasium (there is a separate booklet available about these), or the baby has been bitten by a poisonous spider.

Be sure anyway, that tragedy will strike at some time or another. And at times like this, it is only natural that the wife will want to spend hours on the telephone while she acquaints her mother or closest friend with the news that this time she is leaving the swine for good. This must inevitably lead to a high telephone bill, and sardonic remarks by the husband in the order of, "Since when has your mother been living in bloody Australia?"

Many couples solve this problem by keeping a piggy-bank next to the telephone. This item, if thrown forcibly at the wall by the husband when he discovers it to contain nothing but hairgrips, will do much to alleviate hurt pride.

Adjusting to each other

Like the mating dance of the praying mantis, marriage is a quadrille or, if you are unfamiliar with old-time dancing, a Palais Glide, in which each partner responds almost unconsciously to a pattern of preconceived movements. Thus it will quickly become established that every time you are watching television together, one partner will keep leaning forward and turning up the volume control a fraction, whereas the other partner will keep leaning forward and turning it down again.

It is best to allow these automatic and largely nervous gestures to become part of the background routine of marriage, so that eventually they are hardly noticed by either side. Open discussion on the lines of, "Wassa-marrer, you got cloth ears or something?" may encourage rather than diminish the tension.

Leaving combs on the dressing table with tufts of hair sticking out of them

See our confidential leaflet, "Leaving screwed-up tissues under the pillow in marriage."

The Wedding Industry

by THELWELL

"She'd like to see some rings."

"How quickly can you do invitations?"

"I see you picked the caterers as last time,

"It's from my ex-husband. An automatic toast-scraper"

"That looks great! Now, what do you fancy for your bridesmaids?"

"Have you any ready sliced?"

e it comes! Bridegroom hasn't turned up, can we make
eductions?"

"That was lovely! Could
you hold him up just
once more?"

The Prime Minister

as seen by the winners of our Children's Painting Competition

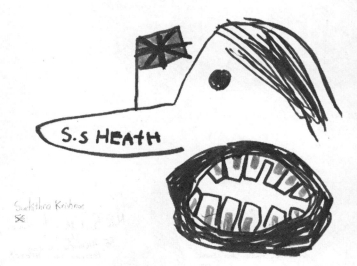

SUCHITHRA KRISHNAN Potters Bar   6 yrs.

CLARE LOOKER Wallington   15 yrs.

Congratulations to Clare Looker who wins the £10 first prize for her study of Mr. Heath, above right, and to the fifteen runners-up who win Poster Chests awarded by Winsor & Newton. As always with drawings by children, the difficulty was in sorting the recognisable portraits from the inspired young freewheelers but we show here a selection of the best entries, picked out by the Editor for their imaginative approach as much as for their likeness to the man himself. Our thanks to all the entrants for their enterprising work.

Ted Heath when young (and old)

JENNIFER CRIPPS Fareham   8 yrs.

ROBIN ROUT Shurdington   14 yrs.

COBDEN Epsom   15 yrs.

BOND Haslemere   12 yrs.

Some Day I'll Find You, Naked as Nature Intended

A new romantic era, says *Time* magazine, is about to hit the screens and bookstalls and drive out permissiveness and violence. Maybe: but ALAN COREN thinks it won't come without a very uneasy transitional period.

CHAPTER VIII Two Hearts Beat As One!

Mrs. Belwether was nervous; and what mother would not be?

She had done their weekend cottage out from top to bottom, and the little house shone like a brass button; the scent of lavender and pine was everywhere, and the rich brown parquet was a mirror of chintz and dimity, and the bright flowers of the spotless curtains, moving gently in the soft spring breeze, were for all the world like the real flowers of her lovely little garden beyond! The horse-brasses winked in the cosy ingle-nook, and the porcelain dog smiled beneath his lampshade, and her collection of reproduction Delft soup-plates sent the friendly rays of the spring sun dancing back into the room, and Crippen the cat sat on the white window-ledge blinking contentedly as he rubbed his furry paws over his fine long whiskers, and the bronz-ette kettle sang happily on the hob. Yes, thought Mrs. Belwether, wonderfully preserved for sixty, I have done *my* bit! Shall I have just a little glass of Stone's Ginger Wine for my palpitations? After all, I *do* deserve it, and it isn't every day that a mummy's only son brings his fiancée home!

She had just washed up the wine-glass and popped a Polo into her mouth when the wheels of Nigel's little two-seater rasped on the gravel, and his horn peep-peeped, the way it always did when he came down to Volehaven from his important job in the city. Hur-riedly, she smoothed her hair. The door chimed gently. She ran to open it.

Nigel stood there smiling, filling the doorway with his fine, lean frame, his handsome face tanned from the drive, his grey eyes twinkling with customary merri-ment.

"Hello, Mumsy!" he said, with his wonderful voice. He put down his cricket bag and his squash racket and

167

his riding-boots and his gleaming twelve-bore, and threw his strong arms around her.

"Hello, darling!" cried Mrs. Belwether. My goodness, she thought, am I really about to weep? Silly old me! "Where's . . ."

Nigel laughed his rich laugh.

"In the car, Mumsy," he replied. "No peeking! I wanted to have you all to myself, just for a minute."

They walked into the parlour, arm-in-arm, and Nigel was about to tell her about his job and his new flat in fashionable Fulham Road, when she slapped his wrist playfully!

"Nigel, I can't wait a moment longer! It really is too naughty of you! Look, there's Father coming in from the radishes now."

"Very well, you silly old thing!" said Nigel, and, with a light laugh, he went out the door.

The lovers returned hand in hand, smiling over some private joke, as lovers will. Mr. and Mrs. Belwether waited by the fireplace.

"Mumsy, Father, this is Julian," said Nigel.

"*The massacres were lyrical enough, but one wasn't left with the sense of shame one had hoped for.*"

They all shook hands. Mr. Belwether, retired from the bank now but still sprightly, poured sherry, and looked Julian up and down, as fathers will.

"So," he said, "this is the young fella who's going to take our little boy away, is it?"

Everyone chuckled! He's so good with people, thought Mrs. Belwether, hugging herself mentally.

"Don't think of it as losing a son, Mr. Belwether," said Julian. "Think of it as gaining a son."

Mrs. Belwether nudged Nigel.

"I think Father wants to be alone with Julian," she said. "Shall I show you my cotoneaster?"

"Right-o!" said Nigel.

When they had gone, Mr. Belwether poured Julian another glass of sherry.

"Now, young fella-me-lad," he said. "This job of yours—pays well, does it? Good prospects?"

Exterior, day. November, a light sleet falling. Trains come and go on Bromley Station, blowing steam, whistling mournfully. Shot of signal, falling limply. Another springs erect. Pan down to station waiting-room, track in on grimy, steamed-up windows, two heads just visible behind glass case of old buns and custard tarts. Close-up of jam sponge with dead fly on it. It goes out of focus, heads sharpen.

Interior, day. Heads belong to middle-aged man (Trevor Howard) and woman (Celia Johnson). They look grave and preoccupied. Pan down from gloomy, distracted eyes to hands on chipped, tea-stained table. The hands edge forward, nervously, touch briefly, and shy away. Track back slowly, to show couple stark naked.

ELIZABETH: We can't go on meeting like this, George. My husband is beginning to suspect.

ACT ONE, Scene One
The hotel balcony. Somewhere, an orchestra is playing *Someday I'll Find You.* The two suites are side by side, and both sets of French windows are open. He emerges from his first, in a velvet smoking jacket, an ivory cigarette holder between his teeth. He is no more than five feet tall, but his bulk is enormous, and the long shaggy hair covering his face seems to make it even larger. There is a large iron bolt projecting from his neck, and a monocle in his one eye. As he stands looking at the moon, and baying softly, she emerges from her suite on to her balcony. They are separated only by a low trellis. She is very tall and slim and white, with waist-length black hair and cool slender arms and two four-inch fangs on either side of her mouth. She is carrying a dripping head, and humming the orchestra's melody softly to herself. After a few moments, he notices her. He licks the saliva from his lips, and smiles, revealing a row of yellow stubs.

HE: I say, isn't that the wine-waiter you've got there?
SHE: Yes, it is, actually.
HE: One always finds the service in Riviera hotels so

"*Richard! I thought we'd turned our backs on suburbia.*"

immeasurably far below that of one's own dear Savoy, doesn't one?

SHE: It was a Dom Perignon '47, and warm as a fresh corpse. What else could I do?

HE: Absolutely nothing, dear lady. Once a foreigner, always a foreigner.

SHE: Ha, ha, ha!

HE: In your position, of course, I should have twisted his head off at the neck. I find finesse unsettling. It should always be left to the vulgar to be elegant, don't you think? They seem to need it so.

SHE: I'm not sure that isn't rather rude.

HE: What do you expect from a werewolf?

SHE: At least you're frank. (*She begins to weep*)

HE: I say, what's up?

SHE: Oh, it's nothing really. I suppose all young gels feel the same way on their wedding night.

HE: I hadn't—I hadn't realised. I'm afraid I took you for Wanda the Lesbian Vampire.

SHE: We look alike, I know—she's fractionally more anaemic—but I'm actually Dracula's Nymphomaniac Daughter Risen From The Grave.

HE: Good lord, you've met Abbot and Costello!

SHE (*Sobbing afresh*): And married them!

HE: My poor child! Dear God, whatever that is, what fools we non-mortals be! What weird coincidence has driven us to share this same moment in destiny?

SHE: You mean, you——

HE: Yes, I too! Forced to an abhorrent nuptial by fate's caprice. Having eaten the rest of the village, I dragged off Olga, the full-breasted virgin, to my filthy lair. But I'm afraid she insisted on a white wedding. I'm not terribly good with women, you know.

SHE: Nor I with men. I had dreamed, one day, of finding a——

HE: Do not speak it!

SHE: Why not? We are here so short a time. I had dreamed of a werewolf, squat and hirsute, someone with whom——

HE: Do you not know that werewolves and vampires never meet? That we are bound to consort only with humans, prey off them alone? I, too, have dreamed!

SHE: Perhaps, in another time . . . (*Sings*) Someday I'll find you——

HE (*Sings*): Moonlight behind you——

(*Orchestra music up, poignantly. They turn slowly, and go inside.*)

CURTAIN

Down memory lane and into the Metropolitan, Edgware Road...

By NED SHERRIN

"If I had known he was going to charge for every prescription he wouldn't have got the damn thing."

The Cambridge School of Undergraduate revue produced a sketch some years ago in which an aged stage door keeper questioned by a suitably nostalgic interviewer about the old timers he had seen launched on a flood of reminiscence.

"I've seen 'em all," he enthused, his eyes misting with tears, "seen 'em all! Florrie Forde, Harry Lauder, Vesta Victoria, Ella Shields, Dan Leno . . . I've seen 'em all . . ." and, pausing suitably, "they was terrible!"

Terrible many of the acts must have been. Hundreds of music halls all over England turning out their local equivalent of today's polythene packed, hygienically wrapped evening of television entertainment. Terrible too was a lot of the life. The legend has mushroomed out of damp dressing rooms, long lay-offs, cold train calls, scratchy orchestras, appalling boarding houses, audiences sometimes silent, or worse, hurling pennies on to dusty stages.

The life of the music hall which fathers the legend was about a hundred years and most of us who feel brushed by its nostalgia have no real idea of what it was like. Old music hall performers always differ in their assessment of performers, material and receptions; but never in the vehemence with which they deny the possibility that a contemporary colleague could be authoritative . . . "of course, he wasn't born then" . . . or "of course she never really was well known—not at the time."

For me the nostalgia starts to prick when I open a book of music hall memories and hear the unmistakable ring of vaudeville prose. The style of magazines like *The Stage*, *The Era*, and *The Referee*, ponderous and self-conscious, colours the heavily jocular pages of the autobiographies.

"Liverpool next claimed my attention," writes Harry Randall (old time comedian); and "Oswald Stoll's migration to Cardiff was the prelude to his multifarious enterprises in the entertainment which culminated in the Stoll Circuit."

It is tempting to think that the excesses of *TV Times* prose will produce comparable biographies of the television age and that dusty covers announcing "Des O'Connor, Old Time Comedian" . . . or "Jimmy Tarbuck; His Book," will inspire a similar thrill of nostalgia in the 2070s.

But will the material have the same romantic ring to it? Putting aside the over loved names, the Marie Lloyds, the Gertie Gitanas the G. H. Elliots and Chirwins, Happy Fanny Fields and Marguerite Broadfoote, a list of footnotes to the history of Variety throws up and defines the tradition more vividly than pages of self-inflicted superlatives in autobiographies. Take these from an American history of Vaudeville.

Chinko, the first man to juggle eight balls and Amerous Werner who juggled ten. Maybell Fonda, the

"I don't know why you race when you're such a damn poor loser."

lady juggler and Charlene and Charlene, two ladies who played the violin while juggling. Acrobats like Boganny's Lunatic Bakers, who jumped in and out of ovens; O. G. Seymour, who jumped over the head of his wife, Kate, and then over an upright piano; and the Bush Brothers who finished with 75 somersaults in a bed.

Strong women and strong men. Martha Farra, who held up a car with twelve men in it while lying on her back on a bed of nails; Apollo, who lifted half a dozen men on a piano. Bertish who arranged for a 250 lb. cannon to fall on his body and Fred Carroll who bit spikes in half. Enoch the "Manfish" who sat in a tank of water, placed a pail over his head and sang, when he wasn't playing trombone in similar circumstances. The Snakeman, The Boneless wonder, and Herman, the Dancing Skeleton. Song and dance acts . . . Pat Rooney and Marion Bent, "The King and Queen of the Waltz Clog dancing," Peg Leg Bates, the Negro Monopede and monopede double acts who, in the interests of economy, made one pair of shoes do for two.

In the 1900s a number of American acts used to travel a group of Negro children who could really sing and dance as "insurance." Grace La Rue had her Inkydinks, Phina, her "Picks." Laura Comstock's "Picanninnies" were three white boys blacked up. Mayme Remington had her Black Buster Brownie Ethiopian Prodigés . . . and Emma Kraus, her Dutch "Picks" (dressed Dutch and singing in German).

Musical acts; Carmenelli & Lucille, "Music and fun in the Butcher's shop," Mlle. Carie, the lady champion Sleigh Bell Player, The Tom-Jack trio who threw snowballs at tambourines set in frames. Tipple and Kelmet who played on wheelbarrows, Ye Colonial Septette, Specht's Lady Serenaders, Binns, Binns and Binns, all made up like King Edward the Seventh, Onaip (which is piano spelt backwards) Jue Fong, "the Chinese tenor," Mlle. Fregoleskas, "the Rumanian Nightingale," Princess Lei Lani, "the McCormack of Hawaii," Sirota, "the Jewish Cantor of Warsaw," Cantor Rosenblatt who finished with "When Irish Eyes are Smiling," and Sissieretta Jones (the Black Patti).

Double acts, Double Irish, Double Dutch, Irish by

name "but Coons by birth," The Mick and the Policeman, the Merry Wop, Two Funny Sauerkrauts.
Female Impersonators, Henry le Clair, "the Sarah
Bernhardt of Vaudeville," Arico Wild, the Male
Melba. Protean Acts, Mimes, Magicians, Hypnotists,
Escapists (Hardeen—Houdini's brother—and Hilda,
the Handcuff Queen), Prelle's Ventriloquial Dogs. The
Curzon Sisters who swung in the air hanging by their
teeth, The Bennett Sisters, who did boxing, fencing and
wrestling. The Weston Sisters, who sang German songs
and boxed. Animal Acts, Dolores Vallecita's Leopards
and Captain Proske's Tigers, Madam Etoile's Society
Horses, Meechams Leaping Dogs, Svengali, the mind-
reading dog, Marzella's Cockatoos, Barnold's Drun-
ken-dog.

It was a world rich in eccentricity. It concentrated a
demanding attention on the performer who held the
small space of stage out there below the gaudily in-
appropriate drop, and it has all gone. I suppose it is
possible that in a hundred years eccentrically named
pop groups like Dozy, Beaky, Mick and Tich or Blod-
wen Pig or Fat Mattress will have a quaintly nostalgic
ring to them but it doesn't sound quite the same
tradition.

Is it to the Northern Clubs that one must look for a
revival? There, just as the original music hall movement grew out of the pubs of South London in particular, entertainers are getting back to the business of
claiming an audience's attention against the rival
attractions of eating and drinking. And if a new music
hall emerges it will throw up some stars and some
terrible acts, some splendid moments and a mass of
misty memories. But it will be harder for the legend to
grow without the background of red plush and gilt and
gas and naphtha and long skirts and brocades and
hackney cabs and the dramatic dashes from hall to hall.
That is the legend I like to believe.

*"I got about 5% less than the extra
20% I demanded which was roughly
what I expected!"*

"Shhh—he's trying to tell us something!"

THE KHRUSCHEV MEMOIRS

ARE THEY GUARANTEED GENUINE? Time/Life thinks so.

ARE THEY A COMPLETE FRAUD? Mrs. Khruschev thinks so.

ARE THEY A PUT-UP JOB BY THE KGB? Everyone else thinks so.

DECIDE FOR YOURSELF!

Here are extracts from four of the Khruschev memoirs that we at Punch have been offered. Using your skill and judgment, place them in what you think is the right order of authenticity.

from IN OUR WAY
by comrade Khruschev

Of all the people I have met, undoubtedly the most outstanding was Joseph Stalin, who on several occasions attempted to assassinate me but otherwise was the most charming and attractive of colleagues. I well remember one occasion when I entered his room just in time to see Kalenovich leaving by the window, which was ten storeys up.

"Kalenovich seems depressed this morning," I remarked.

Stalin smiled and broke his ruler in two.

"He was plotting against me," he said. "I could sense it in my moustache. My moustache never lets me down."

He looked at me strangely, and fingered his moustache. Quickly I put my file on his desk.

"Have a look at this report," I said. "I think your moustache will find it very interesting."

"Perhaps I was wrong," said Joseph, "perhaps Kalenovich was a good boy really." He went to the window and looked out. "We shall never know now."

I left while his back was turned. We have a saying—When the shepherd looks hungry, the sheep dream about lamb chops.

from WHAT I DID IN MY CAREER
by Khruschev N.

I am a party official. Once I was the most important party official in Russia. I did a lot of talking but not much writing, so these memoirs will be quite short. In our country we say, the wolf who barks never catches anything.

My main idea was to get the Americans drunk at parties so they would say silly things. After a while they could do silly things without drinking. We caught one of their planes over Russia. How we laughed!

But then we got drunk and tried to put rockets in Cuba. I think I wrote a silly letter to President Kennedy. And I took my shoe off and banged a table at the United Nations. My colleagues did not believe me when I said I was showing my contempt for capitalist tables. After a while they said, take a rest, Nikita, and they were not smiling. Ah, well. I remember now, we have a saying: man who takes his shoe off in public must have clean socks. Funny, though; we did not have that saying then.

Tomorrow I will get drunk again and write more memoirs.

from THE MAKING OF THE DICTATOR 1956, 1957, ETC, compiled by himself

Our election campaign was based on three basic appeals to the public. One, we are your leaders and you're stuck with us.

Two, we shall increase production targets for everything, especially for jokes about modern art. Three, watch it. To give the public their due, this emotive message packaging really got home to them.

Naturally, my rise to power was in great part due to skilful manipulation of the media. We were lucky enough to win complete control over television, radio, press, advertising and torture, while the opposition's campaign was limited almost entirely to a couple of graffiti in the Moscow suburbs, which were quickly dealt with.

By we, of course, I mean myself and Bulganin. People have often asked me why I chose him as running mate. Would it not have been more sensible, they ask, to find someone about the same size as me? Image-wise this may be true, but it must be remembered that in Russia we like to elect our rulers in pairs so that the mutual suspicion guarantees a balance of power. Bulganin never thought I, a short, chubby person, could constitute a threat. How wrong he was I shall show next week. Can you send the money, please, in a plain envelope to Box 1812 Moscow? Was this the sort of thing you wanted? Ta.

from TEARS 'N LAUGHTER!
An old-stager's story

So that was it! The great day had come! For thirty years I'd been bashing the boards of old Russia, doing one night stands in more places than you've had cold scraps, and suddenly I get the royal command (oops! . . . I mean, the grand soviet command)—Nikita Khruschev is invited to perform on Sunday Night at the Presidium! Talk about laugh! I was scared out of my wits!

Well, I'd known plenty of performers, you see, who'd been shot to stardom in Moscow and then been shot. Remember Beria? He'd worked out a completely unique act with vanishing ladies and trunks and things, which we thought would run for ever, then suddenly—collapse of stout party member! I tell you, I was as nervous as a kitten during a meat shortage.

But everything turned out all right on the night. I told them the one about Eisenhower and the virgin lands, did a few gags like "Pardon me, are those the Urals?" ("No, it's down the passage and first on the left") and finished up with me song: "Not Balalaika-ly!" It was just my usual act but it went down a treat, landing me a ten year contract with an option on an American tour. All doors were open for me, if only I could get rid of my straight man, Bulganin, and go solo.

(Next week: I meet the Queen!)

Now say in not more than ten words why Khruschev made a better George Brown than George Brown and send your entry to us not later than the publication of Nasser's first rush-released biography.

All Quiet
on the Gozo Front

NICHOLAS MONSARRAT buys his way out

On a rainy day in the Channel Islands, with the temperature at forty-seven, the roof leaking, the walls of our bungalow sweating salt spray from the sea (mind you, I've nothing against the Channel Islands except what I've just said), we decided on Malta, in pursuit of the sun and a possible book.

We flew to Malta, and looked round for a house. We looked round, instead, at masses of people in funny hats, new hotels as far from Maltese architecture as a tin of biscuits is from a wedding cake, "holiday flats" sprouting like pale yellow mushrooms, and whole hillside-acres of villas, all costing £15,000.

We looked at one of those decorative horse-drawn carriages with splendid harness and a linen canopy. They are called *karrozzin*, I now know; but I did not know it then, and I wanted to find out. I approached the driver, standing on the street corner, and pointed: "What is that called?"

"Horse," he said.

We decided on Gozo, the small "sister isle" about three miles away. On Gozo we laid down certain immutable guide-lines. The house was to be small. Just a shack on the beach. Right at the water's edge. Impossible to spoil. *No* spare room. And not a penny over £3,000.

We had a week to choose, and the week ran out quickly. Nothing, we found, cost £3,000 except ruined mansions which would need another £5,000 to restore them. There were no secluded shacks on beaches; every beach was already booked solid.

There *was* one mean slit of a house, beautifully perched above a harbour. £10,000. There was a *boat-house* at the water's-edge, but that would need a building permit to convert. And lots of money. And, say, a year.

Only inland were there any of the sort of small house we wanted. My dreams of paddling at dawn, beachcombing at noon, fishing off the front porch, keeping a boat at anchor right under my eyes, all evaporated. Meanwhile, our guide, mentor, and part-time estate agent, Mr. Xerri, was losing heart.

"At such a price," he said—and clearly he did not think much of our price, "you can only hope for a small farm-house in a village." A farm-house, we now realised, did not mean a *farm-house*; it was a cottage in which all the animals, from goats to rabbits, lived on the ground floor, and their owner slaves one floor above them. Mr. Xerri did not think this mode of life really suitable for us, and showed it in various ways.

"Do you know Commander Bannister?" he would ask. "He has this big house, with eight canes!" "Canes" was a measure of land, not yet determined by us. "He was one of my clients."

I had to say that I did not know Commander Bannister. "But he is in the Navy!" said Mr. Xerri, astounded. I had the impression that if Barclays Bank (DCO) had not introduced us to Mr. Xerri, we would be deeply suspect. Once, in the same pursuit of determining, or perhaps improving, our status, he had pointed to a pinkish, fattish man in bulging blue shorts,

with the look of a decayed bloodhound about him.

"That is the Honourable Banks!" he whispered. "Son of the Earl of—" and he named the man responsible. "Do you know him?"

"No."

"But he is English!"

"Well . . ."

"He was one of my *first* clients," said Mr. Xerri. "A new villa. With four *tumoli* of land!"

Once he said: "If you stay—" and already he sounded doubtful, "you will join the British Residents' Association. They meet once a week to discuss death duties."

At 7 p.m. on our last night, when we had abandoned all hope, Mr. Xerri called for us at the hotel. "There is a little house at San Lawrenz," he said. "A small village in the west. It has been converted already."

"How much?" I asked.

"I think £5,000."

"How much land?"

Mr. Xerri's eyes gleamed in the half dark. "Two *mondelli*!"

We drove westwards through increasing twilight. Once Mr. Xerri pointed downhill. "There is a well known island there," he said. "It is called *Il Gebla tal-General*. You would call it Fungus Rock."

It was, indeed, a little house; two up, two down, but built like a rock of honey coloured stone, tiled where it should be tiled, with a tall courtyard and (though we could only guess in the darkness) a marvellous view of the sea, all round and a mile away. But it was semi-detached, clipped to the tiny cottage next door.

"What about that?" I asked Mr. Xerri. "Is it for sale as well?" It was just the sort of little house which people suddenly convert into one of those damned holiday flats: I had visions of week-end parties, people making love *and* war all night, guitars, beads, fringed maxi-boots, everything.

"I believe so," said Mr. Xerri. "If you are interested in this one."

In the pitch-darkness of the courtyard I conferred with my wife, in the sense that I said "What do you

*"But Her Grace was only supposed to make a **small** hole for the tree."*

think?" and she said, "Yes," and I said "All right, let's go." We returned to Mr. Xerri, feeling absolutely round the bend already. It was nine p.m. when we said "Yes" to him. But: "There is a *nutar* waiting," he said.

The village electricity had failed, and it was by waving lamplight that the deed was done. Notary Buttigieg, who had read one of my books and seemed astonished at our purchase, wrote the contract out in long-hand. I was "Nicholas, son of the late Keith and the late Marguerite"; my wife was "Ann, daughter of the living Cyril and the living Marie Patricia." Our house was named as 92 Dalelands Street.

"Subject to perpetual ground rent," Notary Buttigieg warned as he wrote in his rounded, laborious script. "Four shillings and fourpence a year. If you do not pay

for three years, the Franciscan Fathers will take the house from you."

"I'll remember." But it reminded me about something else. "What about the little house next door? Is that for sale?"

Notary Buttigieg knew all about this. "Yes. But it is a question of the hairs. There are seven hairs, and one in Australia, and one who cannot communicate. It will take some time."

"I'd like to have the first refusal."

His spectacles dropped. "You *refuse* the house?"

"No. I would like to make the first offer for it."

"That will be noted. . . . You should sign the contract here."

We gave him ten per cent down, and a full power of attorney as well, just as the lamp went out.

It might have been crazy, but it was not, even though a letter arrived, a week later, saying: "Your house would rather be called No. 15 Triq il-Wileg." Indeed, it was downhill all the way, compared with what we feared, or had heard from desperate friends on the Costa Brava, who had been trapped with empty building sites, villas half constructed and then abandoned, other villas which appeared, almost overnight, ten yards in front of their picture window, drains unconnected, water like fluoride blood.

We had an architect to organise a few alterations. He was a cheerful optimist. When anything did not fit,

or was lop-sided, he said: "We'll make a feature of it." Our house is full of such features. The narrow louvred swing-doors which snap shut on every passing bottom excite plenty of comment. The water heater in the sitting room is particularly admired.

But the men of Gozo are marvellously willing workmen. When a man arrives to put in a new plug point, he is first a stone mason chipping away to make a channel for the wires. Then he is an electrician, connecting them up. Then he turns into a plasterer, filling in the channel again. Then he is a painter, making all neat and tidy. Lastly he is a housekeeper, with a dustpan and brush, removing all traces.

Try that on the ETU.

Above all, he does not want to be paid. "I come later," he says. If pressed, he puts his hands firmly behind his back. The man who came to build the garden wall was particularly unwilling to take our money on the spot. As my wife advanced with four pound notes, he slowly retreated the whole length of the garden. "No," he said. "I love you." Then he whistled up his dog, and almost ran away.

When our household goods arrived, half the village turned out to watch them being unloaded. They were not impressed; why should they be, by crates of books and saucepans and a few bits of sea-side furniture? But there was one great success: my radiogram, of which I am not proud—it makes a marvellous noise, but looks like something from a hotel lobby in Las Vegas. Yet the murmur of approval swelled, and brought even the children running.

On our first full day as occupants, I got up with the dawn. Outside my window there was a truly magnificent view: a fertile valley, a lighthouse still blinking as it warred with the day, a sparkling sea, and soon a most wonderful luminous sunlight over everything. Fishermen and farmers were just plodding back from first Mass.

Then came the callers. First the dustman, who is also the road-sweeper. How many times a week should he call? We settled for Mondays, Wednesdays, and Fridays. Then there were children with flowers, old ladies with presents of eggs and turnips and beans, and a man who wanted to lend me a hoe until I had one of my own.

At nine a.m. there was a sudden stern cry of "Nicholas!" from the other side of the courtyard wall. I was nervous: it sounded just like my mother. But when I opened the door, it was the village policeman.

"You are Nicholas?" he asked. And when I said that I was: "The telephone wants you," he said. "Come to my station."

At ten o'clock it was the postman on a motorcycle. He handed me a crested, embossed envelope. "It is an invitation from the Governor General," he told me beaming. "I think you are an important man."

I felt so already.

". . . and confined you will remain until such time as you are fit to be seen among civilised people."

Do I Own Billy Smart's Circus?

By BASIL BOOTHROYD

There are people with a keen sense of property and people without: those who keep their money in tray-purses and buttoned hip-pockets, and those who couldn't tell you, from one day to the next, whether they'd carve up at the final, grim accounting for a round £40,000 or £11.50p. I belong to the last lot, and it's catching. When I once asked my son—not to say heir—why he'd come home for the holidays without his bicycle, and he said, "It went under a tractor," we both considered the matter closed.

All the same, even I begin to feel a twinge of alarm at the way Whitehall's been shuttling my possessions about. Naturally, it's no help not to have any reliable record of what my possessions are, and I think governments may take advantage of that. I'm clear about the railways. I fancy they gave me those in 1948, though I may be thinking of the time they took India away. It was certainly nice to have 33,000 miles of track and all those fretwork platform canopies grabbed off the bloated LNER etc. shareholders and presented to me, but privileges bring responsibilities: I must readily accept the blame for having lost a lot of track, stations and money during my twenty-odd years of ownership. Looking back, I don't know what I was thinking of, letting things slide like that.

I gather that, at the time of going to press, I've still got the Post Office, or at least the non profit-making parts. Also the gasworks, and those electricity showrooms

*"That's where the Commies have the edge on us—they don't
have to worry about the Dow-Jones index."*

where painfully pink plastic cutlets lie enticingly in the open cookers, and the staff
stand at a distance in preoccupied knots until customers go away. The last I heard,
the British Steel Corporation's still mine. It's been tough to find that £22,500 a year
for Chairman Melchett—though no tougher than keeping my airline pilots happy
since they were made over to me in 1967, and all those hostesses shrilling away about
their free tights—but it's been pleasant to wander around Scunthorpe or Port Talbot
knowing I've got a finger in those terribly old tatty red-hot buckets they swing
around in the BBC2 colour test films. There used to be an old ballad, in waltz time
and three flats, that must have been about steel:

    "I had you, I lost you, I found you . . .
    Only to lose you again . . ."

But the truth is, as far as I'm concerned, that whether I've had it, lost it, found it or
(as seems likely) lost it again, it doesn't seem to have affected me much in terms of
whether I could afford to have the house rewired or get the grandfather clock
mended. The position, as I see it, is that whether steel belongs to me under the
Socialists, or a lot of little old well-breeched ladies in Sunningdale, under the Tories,
it would take a sharp bank manager to detect related fluctuations in my financial
standing. I've no doubt it's my own fault. On the other hand, you can worry too
much. If I'd been a tray-purse man, all that nash, de-nash, re-nash and re-de-nash
could have had me in the Maida Vale Hospital for Nervous Diseases before now.
It takes it out of you, having a whole industry arrive on your doorstep, gift-wrapped
from Attlee, snatched back by Macmillan, dumped again by Wilson, whipped again
by Heath. And I don't know, incidentally, how the accountancy side goes with this
kind of thing, but I can't help feeling that a few blast furnaces and sheet finishing
plants rub off on the middle-man each time. Not that I miss them, I suppose, in
transactions on that scale. Anyway, I see that next time I lose the Corporation it'll
take with it the £283,000,000 it owes me. Even I can appreciate that this was money
I was never going to get, so good riddance to the whole thing, and I'll stop teasing
myself . . .

What I'd prefer to make a point of is that allauning remark by Frank Alarm the other day—sorry, you get confused—when he accused Heath's men of "looting the public's assets." I only wish I could remember which of my assets he was on about. Could hardly have been Rolls Royce, because if I've got things right at all, Rolls Royce is going the other way, being given to me, or at any rate lent (the only sound is the clocking of the tick); and that's odd, in a way, because I always had that *feeling*, if you know what I mean, that if there was one thing I did own, together with the Monarchy, St. Paul's Cathedral and the Peak District National Park, it was Rolls Royce. Now that I'm really going to own it or parts of it (I'll take the cars, anyone can have those RB-211s), in the monetary and material sense, rather than the prestigious and patriotic, I feel it as more of a blow than a benefaction. What you've never had you can't miss, they say, but it doesn't seem to work in this case. It will be the same, no doubt, when they nationalise St. Paul's, on the ground that I can't run the place without letting a lot of cracks develop in its south portico.

Sir Christopher Wren
Said "I'm going to dine with some men,
If anyone calls,
Say I'm repairing St. Paul's."

You can get doctrinaire, if that's the word, over these things. Given an inner conviction that you own a cathedral, whether standing up or falling down, you don't care to have it taken away from you, even for its own good. The same goes for travel agencies. Although Messrs. Thomas Cook and Son have been my property in a more cold-blooded, or book-keeping, sense than Christopher Wren's leaning tower of Ludgate Hill, I still react with warmth to the news that I'm going to be looted of it. If with less warmth than I should have done if I'd known I owned it in the first place. I don't know when Wilson gave me Thos. Cook. I think I must have been on

"*Lot thirty-four. A banana crate once in the possession of Paul Gauguin.*"

holiday at the time, and missed it. Anyway, I see it's being bid for by "a consortium of business men," so there goes my last chance of taking a top brass attitude with the Cook's man next time I find myself in an unfinished hotel in Ibiza. "If this is the best way you can run my company . . ." "Send me the manager on bended knees . . ." "You're fired." The business men may get the thing on to a profit-making footing, but what does that do for me? I've been looted, and that's it. They'll be looting me of the coal mines next, and that'll be the end of my long, self-satisfied gloat over possessing all those picturesque South Wales slagheaps.

Personally, I'm going to turn over a new leaf and try to be a bit more responsible, finding out, for a start, just what my assets are. Have they given me Woolworth's yet? Jodrell Bank? The MCC? If so, there's the diversification problem. Wheels within wheels. If the laundry industry is mine, it could mean that I own a piece of its brickworks, surgical instruments concerns, nutmeg interests. Am I in fact dialling my own number when I call up a pregnancy-testing consortium to say I don't like the style of its advertising in my underground trains? And, if so, just what agonies of deprivation will rack me when I read that the whole thing, with its worldwide litmus-paper installations, is to be looted off me and turned over to money-grubbing private enterprise?

In my present state of ignorance, that one's easily answered. What agonies? No agonies. It's knowing that's going to hurt, and I must brace myself for that. The day I find that I own Tom Jones, Crawley New Town, the Midland Red bus company and Dr. Collis Browne's Chlorodyne, to name a few, I shall be on watch for looters by day and night. So thank you, Frank. When they come down the street, yelling and smashing windows and carrying off my Bank of England, or whatever it is, I shall try to put up a fight that's worthy of you.

Anyway, that's what I feel at the moment. I don't say that if they leave me a decent Rolls outside I mightn't weaken.

"Thank God! He's turning off at last."

Drinking Songs for Very Rich Men

by PETER DICKINSON

THE THREE OLD MEN

I'll sing you a song of a rich old man
Who (poor old man) put a total ban
    On liquor, but being wealthy
He spent an enormous amount of dough
In a search for the purest H_2O.
    He found it. It tasted filthy.
CHORUS: He wasn't our sort like we're our sort.
        Bring on the dancing girls! Pass the port!

I'll sing you a song of a rich old man
Who (poor old man) was a puritan.
    His notion of wicked living
Was owning a great pink Renoir nude
Which once a year he unveiled and viewed
    With a sort of baffled misgiving.
CHORUS: He wasn't our sort like we're our sort.
        Bring on the dancing girls! Pass the port!

I'll sing you a song of a rich old man
Who (poor old man) was a health-food fan.
    The victuals upon his table
Were brown bread baked from a hand-milled wheat
From a humus farm—and of that he'd eat
    As little as he was able.
CHORUS: He wasn't our sort like we're our sort.
        Bring on the dancing girls! Pass the port!

Now these three old fellows they all went bust
Through choosing the wrong companions to trust.
    (Have I mentioned they weren't our sort?)
We've solved that problem with minimum fuss,
For none of us trust any of us,
    Excepting to pass the port.
CHORUS: For you are my sort like I'm your sort.
        Bring on the dancing girls! Pass the port!

———————◆———————

WINE AND/OR WOMEN

Woman, as every schoolboy knows,
    Assorts but ill with wine.
Her cheek may be the scented rose,
    Her embonpoint divine.
        (Far gone, far gone the diner able
        To see much more—beneath the table.)
But oh, the odour of that rose,
    The heaving of that chest,
Confounds the senses, fills the nose—
    What wine can stand the test?
        I learned this wisdom from my father
        Who told me, nothing loth,
        "Enjoy whichever you would rather
        But don't, my son, try both."

Love of good wine, each housewife knows,
    Is not so good for love.
How often does some lad propose
    Some lassie's worth to prove
        (Selecting her because the wine
        Has somehow made the wit resign.)
But she, when tempted to his cell
    With maidenly demur,
Finds he who does himself too well
    Does not so well with her.
        I learned this wisdom from my granny:
        "They both are worth the bother,
        But if you'd be a Man, my mannie,
        You must choose one or other."

Now we, as all assembled know,
    Have made a useful hoard
And rare indeed is the Chateau,
    Or girl, we can't afford.
        But still we face this problem which
        Afflicts the poor man and the rich.
Let us resignedly carouse,
    Forgetting love's delight.
This is the night, my friends, to souse—
    To-morrow's Ladies' Night.
        I learned this wisdom from my mother:
        I teach it to my sons:
        "Choose sometimes one and sometimes t'other,
        But never both at once."

———————◆———————

OLD CITY TOAST

Here's a health unto the Chancellor
    (*with a fal fiddle lal and whistle for a wind*)
Who brings new notions by the score
To rescue the Economee
And foists them on the Treasuree
    (*with a fal fiddle lal and whistle for a wind*)

Here's a health unto the Treasuree
    (*with a ho hum hum and wait another year*)
They've dealt before with such as hee.
They tell him that it can't be done
And pray that soon he will be gone.
    (*with a ho hum hum and wait another year*)

Here's a health to him and a health to them
    (*with a rum dumble dum and what's in it for me*)
If they leave in peace poor businessmen.
May the Chancellor soon be made a Lord
And the Civil Servant sit on our board.
    (*with a rum dumble dum and what's in it for me*)

181

Natty Gents Nudity

By LORD ARRAN

I do not wear gear: at my age it is unbecoming and the young do not respect the old who try to be with it. But I confess that I wish I could. Monsieur Poisson once gave me two silk evening shirts and I get quite a kick when I come into the drawing-room before dinner. "Look at me": I say to my hostess. "Aren't I trendy? Aren't I real groovy?" And she smiles politely, though I know that the young guests are thinking "cool it man. You're way out? You look like Father Goose."

Yes, I like gear but gear does not like me. I also like minis, but I am told that once again I am not with it. Minis are grotty. It is all so difficult. My father decided at fifty that henceforward he would only wear double-breasted blue suits with a blue shirt, an open wing collar and a black tie, wherever he was and whatever he was doing. He looked uncommonly smart, and he never needed to go to the tailor or the hosier.

With me alas it is different. I vary between eleven and thirteen stone and I am constantly experimenting. Ties are really exciting nowadays. I have big floppy ones and sometimes with an open collar I feel positively Byronic though I have no neck.

I also grow my hair a little longer to my grown-up sons' surprise and dislike. Short back and sides for them. And then my new flared trousers! I shudder to think of my Oxford bags.

But I can still startle. My 1930 correspondents, brown and white of course, at the village fête set eyes goggling. The young were positively outraged. Nakedness might have shocked the vicar and the lady bountiful. But no one else. Even my grandfather's German Uhlan uniform and decorations—he fought at Sadowa in 1867—would have been not a hundred but, far worse, five years out of date.

I deplore this trend towards nudity—and after the Isle of Wight it seems to be moving that way. Moreover it is a very bad thing for industry. The man's hatters never fully recovered from the news that fresh air keeps hair healthy, and though with our present pavements it is unlikely, the BMA have only to condemn shoes as bad for the toes and conducive to smelly feet—which they are—for Mr. Clore to have to think up something new. I tremble to think of what we should lose in exports if there were no home-market for British suits and shirts and kilts, and we stopped making them.

Imagine for a horrible moment, Britain, in a few short years' time, as one vast nudist colony. Before leaving the ship or the aeroplane you go to the undressing room, for no one may land with a stitch of clothes on (back to hats for a moment: hats *might* be permissible). You have no luggage, so you have no customs except the suspects who are given a rather special examina-

"I'm sorry, he's in conference at the moment!"

"If it wasn't for the omnipotence, I think I'd jack the whole thing in."

tion. It is raining, but of course mackintoshes are out, though an umbrella is permissible if held well above the head. The kisses between relations at least are somewhat more self-conscious and restrained, the comments too. "You've put on a little weight, Auntie," says sonny boy glancing at her midriff, "and you never told us you've had an operation." The greetings between lovers will be in a special room, though they will not be much used.

For due to the cheapening of the currency, sex is now so ridiculous that it has been made compulsory to keep humanity alive. There are "blue" films showing people in clothes, and stripteases starting with neat flesh and working up to an orgastic full morning coat; but to be caught looking is as bad as to be caught eating in Arab countries during Ramadan and, as there, involves imprisonment.

Life indeed seems strangely uninteresting. There is little scope for originality, and somehow even rooms don't look right. Flesh does not fit easily into a colour-scheme, and furniture has to be designed without protruding corners or sharp edges. It is permissible to dye the skin any colour, but the danger persists of sitting on a sofa which clashes with your particular shade of woad.

Sport, too, especially the more manly team-sports can be dangerous though the absence of boots and hard balls lessens the risk, and mixed hockey is illegal. But generally the trend is towards unisex, and, of course, marriage for those who go in for that sort of thing can be between any two persons.

Children can be bought, but they are very expensive and the tendency is to buy them for the colour of their skins. "It looked sweet, darling, but with the new red Mini it was hopeless. I mean, cars first, kids afterwards."

And then there's the problem of animals. It was only by the narrowest of parliamentary margins that sheep were allowed to grow wool. "An affront to progress," Harold Wilson IV called it, and there are many who agree though the attempt to enforce the compulsory plucking of all cats' hairs was rightly defeated. In the world of art, the feeling is growing that though pink is nature's colour, you can have too much of a good thing, and really there is something to be said for keeping grass green.

Last this question of cold. People, particularly old people, feel the cold; even among the most hide-bound of naturists, this is admitted. It can also lead to ill-health, though the growth of protective fur has helped. In despair, a non-party resolution has been adopted allowing men and women over sixty to stay in bed permanently and also "those whose physical appearance is such as to cause distaste among others and likely to detract from the ideals of body-worship."

"Britain is bare and boring and bankrupt," said Lord Arran, now a hundred and four years old and living in Paris: "To think that I should have to live abroad among a lot of damned foreigners to keep my clothes on."

At home with

THE FIVE FLYING FOGARTYS

by LARRY

Which?

The Dennis J. Rossington

The Dennis J. Rossington Family Model was first tested twenty-three years ago, when it was found to be quite passable. It had a top speed of thirty mph, went up fairly smoothly through the gears, and its steering was remarkably precise. Its indicators worked well, it handled carefully in the wet, and the attention to minute detail was found to be very commendable, if a trifle fussy. Four adults could be driven long distances in relative comfort, and parking was exceptionally good. We decided to test the Dennis J. Rossington one hundred thousand miles later, to see how well this popular model had stood up to the passage of time.

Finish

On the surface, not too bad: the bodywork beneath the outer coats, however, had become considerably distorted and a somewhat unnerving shake had developed, particularly in the hands. It was heavier on Scotch than it used to be, and far noisier. Tell-tale lines were beginning to develop around exposed protuberances, and there was a disturbing central sag.

Performance

More serious deterioration here. It still started well enough, and was quite good on short trips, although even on these we found the steering to be imprecise, the braking sharp and snatchy, and the gear-changing fierce and rough. On longer journeys, however, some terrifying faults emerged: on motorways in particular, it rapidly overheated and began making shocking noises, especially when passed by anything. It tended to accelerate in fog, for some weird reason our experts were unable to determine. Its indicator system broke down completely, its lights flashed constantly, its steering was horrifying, and it kept going pink. Water leaked from all pores. At the end of such runs, parking was impossible, achievable only by barging into other things and leaving the back wheels on kerbs.

Conclusions

The Dennis J. Rossington is no longer roadworthy.

The Hon. Gaveston Pune-Futtering

Known to its few admirers as Old Futters, this intriguing hand-built special is the product of centuries of individual attention and is in consequence not only almost obsolete but also utterly impossible to handle. A fortune has been spent on finish, but nothing has been done to the basic works since time immemorial, and our testers had no hesitation in labelling it a death-trap and a threat to everything else on the road.

Finish

No mass-production here. The Hon Gaveston Pune-Futtering is covered in hundreds of layers of glossy, impenetrable coating. Long and undeniably sleek, it does, however, have a virtually imperceptible profile. It looks its best when motionless, parked outside Annabel's.

Performance

The first thing to be remarked about this model is its incredible noisiness: it cannot drive without over-revving, it cannot pass without honking (ours had a four wind-horn assembly which played *Colonel Bogey,* but you can also get *Glory Glory Hallelujah, D'ye Ken John Peel?* and *Selections From Verdi's Requiem*), and it cannot park without going "Haw! Haw! Haw!" and slamming its doors, especially at three in the morning. It is at its most typical when driving the wrong way round Sloane Square at sixty (in second gear) or flashing V-signs at bus-drivers whom it has just cut up and using its expensive speed to avoid the consequences. It is immeasurably expensive to run, since it requires constant topping up with Dom Perignon '47 and, due to its accident proneness, is impossible to insure, except through its father, who owns much of Lloyd's. It usually has female passengers who go "Hee! Hee! Hee!" when it goes "Haw! Haw! Haw!"

Conclusions

The Hon. Gaveston Pune-Futtering is no longer roadworthy.

The Miss Phoebe Wicket, B. Mus.

The Miss Phoebe Wicket, B. Mus. o appears on roads during rush hours and only in the fast lane, at 18 mph, its top speed. It is not always easy t spot, since its habit, being tiny, is to crouch over the wheel, peering thro it, occasionally disappearing from s altogether to pick up a fallen harp, music manuscript, teaching schedu bottles of Scott's Emulsion, shoppin or the cat. At such moments, it is most easily distinguishable by its wobbling and the scraping noise it makes when sideswiping other vehic If it runs into you, it smiles. Sometim it waves as well.

Finish

Somewhat frail in appearance, yet w found it to have a strange toughnes that enabled it to stand up amazingl well after the eleven collisions it had during our brief test run. On one occasion, having come to a halt against the confectionery counter in the British Home Stores, Palmers Green, it remained utterly unmarked and merely ordered a quarter of cherry nougat.

Performance

We found the performance of the Miss Phoebe Wicket, B. Mus. to be virtually non-existent: it refused to reverse, it refused to overtake, it refused to give any signals whatever it refused to turn on its lights, and it could only be persuaded to change gear when the labouring of the engin was such as to rattle the windows o of their frames. It avoided turns as much as possible, and tended not to go anywhere that wasn't in a straigh line from where it had been before. Instead of braking, it merely ran slowly into the thing in front—bus, wall, policemen, whatever happened to be convenient at the time. It took nine hours to get to Birmingham in t fast lane of the M1, singing all the w The windscreen wipers were going throughout, although there wasn't a cloud in the sky.

Conclusions

The Miss Phoebe Wicket, B. Mus. is no longer roadworthy.

"Pay attention to the game, will you!"

PUNCH'S A TO Z FRENCH COURSE

By DAVID WILLIAMS

A is for Amour, which these days the French don't seem to be going in for quite as much as we do. In the singular it's masculine (un amour permanent); in the plural it's feminine (des amours imperman-entes). If this means anything it's presumably that the French consider the women to be the ones with a roving eye.

B is for Bon, which means good, though not always. They say "Ah bon!" in a tone of surprise quite a lot, and this means "I see what you mean." Thus "Ah bon! Tu veux dire que Tonton est au bagne" means "Oh I see. You mean Nunky's in the nick" —after somebody's been roundabout breaking it to you.

C is for Coup, which can mean almost anything. Un coup de rouge is a snifter of wine. Tu as raté le coup means you've missed the boat. Don't look "Coup" up in the dictionary. That way madness lies.

D is for Dis donc, which is simply a noise calling attention to yourself. English equivalent roughly "Oi."

E is for Est-ce-que (Esker) and means answer my question. Est-ce que tu vas me payer un verre? Are you going to buy me a drink?

F is for Foutre, which is eff as in eff off only slightly less rough. Thus an enthusiastic Toulouse rugby fan might say X optimistically half way through the second half of the Toulouse-Harlequins match: Les Harlequins sont foutus, or The Harlequins are

buggered. This might well be far from the truth.
(See my tingling book *Forward Play in the Garonne
Valley*.)

G is for Gare, the place where the trains arrive infal-
libly on time and where the buffet can almost
always be relied upon for a good, relatively in-
expensive, nosh. See also Chef de Gare, meaning
stationmaster, or one whose wife is repeatedly un-
faithful (see Amours, feminine). "Il est cocu, le
Chef de Gar-e." Sing this.

H is for Hein, a frequently used noise meaning
roughly: Agree with what I've just been telling
you. To pronounce: say "air" down your nose.
We'll take a break now for you to try this.

*   *   *

I is for Il y a, pronounced ya. Start your sentences
with this: it launches them like a bottle of Bollinger
whanged against the backside of a million-ton
tanker. "Il y a une gonzesse dans mon potage"—
—"There's a girl in my soup." (I think.)

J is for Jambon (ham as in ham sandwich). The
French ham sandwich is not recommended to those
taking the course. It's craggy, often fatal to false
teeth and bread is to jambon as interval is to play
during wet Saturday afternoon cricket matches.

K is not worth bothering with unless you are going to
Brittany where you might run into Korrigans
(fairies) at the bottom of your garden or even right
up under the kitchen sill, only you'd need to put
your head well out of the window to see them
because they don't come in large sizes (around one
foot four in a good season).

L is for Lecture, which doesn't mean lecture as you
might think, but reading. Lecture is conférence.
This goes some way towards showing that in French
things aren't always what they seem. Thus corres-
pondance doesn't mean correspondence but a
station on the Metro where two lines intersect,
enabling you to change. (Only there'll be a long,
long trail down white-tiled corridors lined with
enamelled placards telling you what to go for if
you've got inflammation of the urinary tract like
Jean-Jacques Rousseau—see my eye-opening book
Down Literary By-ways.)

M is for Monsieur, which is not, as English novelists
make out, pronounced M'sieu. It's pronounced
Merse Year (the "ea" as in yearn). Raymond
Queneau spells it Meussieu and he ought to know.

N is for n'est-ce pas, pronounced spaw. Immensely
useful, this, as you can keep on saying it, *without
doing any harm at all to your general drift*, until you've
thought of the word you want to continue with.

O is for Oh là là (pronounced Oh-là—slight pause
then resume one tone down—là!) meaning Cor!
We'll take another break here for practice.

*   *   *

P is for pronunciation in general. Stay with me now
because this will take some time. Basic stuff only
then:
1. English comes from the back of the throat,
   French from the front of the mouth. When an
   Englishman says "Pa" he gargles. When a
   Frenchman says "Papa" it's a quick sharp
   sound like corks coming almost simultaneously
   out of a couple of bottles of Moët et Chandon.
2. "U" is like nothing we have over here. Say "ee"
   with the inside of your mouth, and then, *holding
   the inside position, adjust the lips, *but lips only*,
   as for whistling. Right. Are you sitting comfortably? Prepare to say: "Jeanne Dubu a perdu
   son tutu." (She's a ballet-dancer, this Jeanne
   Dubu, but stripping is infiltrating everywhere.)
3. "R." The thing to do with "R" is stick south of
   a line drawn horizontally through Brive-la-
   Gaillarde. Then you should be OK provided
   you let the tongue r-rip. *North* of that line you're
   in dead trouble, but try to manage a voiced
   gargle with no spit. All right? Pass on then.
4. *Vowels in general*. Keep these as pure as a Mother
   Superior keeps her novices. Difficult this, because English vowels are as impure as conversation in a windjammer's foc's'le thirty days out of
   Hull and waiting still for the roaring forties.
   N.B. An impure vowel is one which doesn't start
   as it means to go on. Are you getting flustered?
   Break off and pop down the road to the nearest
   arterial caff, and listen to a lorry-driver from

Ynysybwl asking for a cup of cocoa. Cocoa will be the word to listen for. Dai the Truck's "o" will start as it means to go on; Dave's from Dagenham will box the compass from "a" to "oo." My urgent call to all French speakers is: *Copy Dai.*

This concludes Pronunciations, nasals having been dealt with under Hein. Take another break now. Rinse your mouth out and spit into the bowl.

* * *

Q is for Quoi qu'il en soit (kwa keel ah—Breathe it down your nose—swa). This means howsomedever and is essential equipment for actors taking smock-frock parts in ORTF telly translations of *Far From the Madding Crowd.*

R is for Reglisse (raygliece, to rhyme with piece). It means liquorice, and if you play your cards properly there's no reason why you shouldn't go through life without having to rake round in your memory for this one.

S is for Si, which means Yes, but *not always.* "You don't believe a word I'm telling you, do you?"—"Oh yes I do." Now that yes'd be si, see? I wonder if you do. Well then, "si" is "yes," when yes comes as a surprise. Does that help?

T is for Tu. Thou hast to watch out with this one, by God thou hast. Theeing and thouing is frequent in French, but strictly controlled unlike our prices and incomes. Our all-purpose "you" shares itself out between "Tu" and "Vous." If a man driving an E-type Jag cuts in in front of you and then brakes sharply you call him "tu." "Ah salaud, qu'est-ce que tu fais?" you ask (Ah saloh, keskertu—remember that "u" business we talked about? fe?—"fe" as in "fetch"). You also say: "Embrasse-moi, chérie. Embrasse-moi vite, tu me fais bander." This means: kiss me you doll, you. You are causing me considerable sexual excitement (yes, I know, there's a shorter way of saying this in English too). Briefly: Tu for fondness, familiarity and fury. Otherwise vous (oo as in soot rather than as in boot).

U We've been into this. Keep whistling.

V is for vin (say "air" down your nose again). This is important, ever present, vital. Don't overdo it though if the stuff is young, as often in monasteries (*why?*) because if you do you may wake up twelve hours later in strange surroundings.

W is for Vécés (vaysay roughly). "Ou sont les vécés?" you ask, if you are one to look ahead, when entering your hotel, and they'll show you a cramped loo (pitch black, no window) with a light that comes on only when you shoot the bolt. How to locate the bolt in the dark? You don't want my French course for this. You want a match (allumette—"u" again, keep at it).

X is for Express which means a train that stops a lot, another instance (c.f. Lecture) of the way in French things aren't always what they seem. While I'm at it I might also mention that it's for Expertise, one of the words we've taken over and given a fresh meaning to. It doesn't mean "expertness" as we seem to think, but "an expert's report" or "valuation." Still, don't let's be fussy, but pass on to

Y is for y which can mean almost anything, but roughly "to it," "to them," or "there"—that sort of thing. Vas-y (vazzee) means get cracking, which is really about all there's left for you to do now, after which you can be in there joking (plaisantant) and ready to hold your own with (tenir tête à) Pompidou.

Z —well, it had better go in, but there's nothing much except *zinc*, the counter in a bistro where you can be supplied with any or all of these splendid drinks they have—Anisette, Byrrh, Cointreau, Dubonnet, St. Estèphe, Fernet Branca, which tastes like gunpowder and is equally explosive in its effects—you could go all through the alphabet again, just sticking to liquor, but before you got as far as S you'd be stoned (saoûl, pronounced soo). And at this point the French Course would run off you like brandy off a canard's back (dos, pronounced to rhyme with Dough, which is one of the occasional words which give us a bit of our own back).

"They are really quite unique sir—we sell a lot of them."

A place in the country

by THELWELL

"It's nice to get away from 'The Smoke.'"

"What on earth do you mean—no stuffed olives?"

"You've got to admit it! They've done a tasteful restoration of their outside privy."

"I'm sorry to bother you! I've run out of liver paté."

Index of Artists

Index of Writers